21st Century Houses

150

of the World's Best

21st Century Houses

150 of the World's Best

Robyn Beaver

images
Publishing

Published in Australia in 2010 by
The Images Publishing Group Pty Ltd
ABN 89 059 734 431
6 Bastow Place, Mulgrave, Victoria 3170, Australia
Tel: +61 3 9561 5544 Fax: +61 3 9561 4860
books@imagespublishing.com
www.imagespublishing.com

National Library of Australia Cataloguing-in-Publication entry
Title: 21st century houses : 150 of the world's best / editor Robyn Beaver.
ISBN: 9781864703818 (hbk.)
Notes: Includes index.
Subjects: Architecture, Domestic—21st century.
                 Architecture, Modern—21st century.
Dewey Number: 728

Designed by The Graphic Image Studio Pty Ltd, Mulgrave, Australia
www.tgis.com.au

Pre-publishing services by Mission Productions Limited, Hong Kong
Printed on 140 gsm Chinese matt art paper by Paramount Printing Company Limited, Hong Kong

IMAGES has included on its website a page for special notices in relation to this and our other
publications. Please visit www.imagespublishing.com.

Contents

1290 Residence and Studio

Amherst, Massachusetts, USA

Sigrid Miller Pollin, FAIA, Architect

Photography: Peter Mauss, Esto and
Tom Bonner

This residence is inspired by the traditional white clapboard farmhouses of New England. It takes its cues from the specifics of the site and a contemporary programmatic mix of spaces for living and working. A sweeping curve connects an art and architecture workspace on the west, a drive-through arbor in the center, and living space on the east. The living/dining space opens up exuberantly to views of the meadow to the east while maintaining privacy with high walls and clerestory windows. The operable clerestory windows on the west and operable view windows on the east provide cross ventilation through the living/dining space. The traditional screen porch at the lower level is reinterpreted with an aluminum frame grid.

The studio/work wing is located perpendicular to the residential spaces. This L-shaped plan forms an entry garden area with a cobblestone driveway that doubles as a patio area. The driveway passes through an arbor designed for climbing, flowering vines and which also acts as a rainwater collector. The project features an abundance of sustainable design components, including radiant heating, bamboo flooring, low-E glazing, rainwater harvesting, natural light and ventilation throughout, high R-value ceiling and floor insulation, and landscaping with native species.

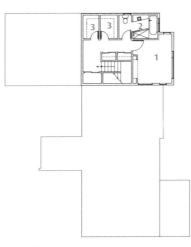

Second floor plan

1 Bedroom
2 Bathroom
3 Storage
4 Sauna
5 Library
6 Screened porch

Third floor plan

1 Master bedroom
2 Master bathroom
3 Closet

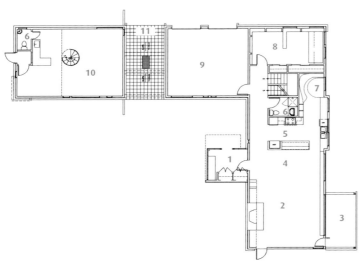

First floor plan

1 Entry
2 Living area
3 Deck
4 Dining area
5 Kitchen
6 Bathroom
7 Built-in banquette
8 Study
9 Garage
10 Studio
11 Courtyard

Alexander Residence

New Orleans, Louisiana, USA

Ken Tate Architect

Photography: Timothy Dunford

The architect likens this house to a New Orleans "gumbo." Like the famous recipe, the 13,000-square-foot residence comprising seven buildings features a mélange of cultures and styles. The porches have the deep overhangs and sturdy Tuscan columns of French West Indies and Louisiana Creole plantation houses; in the living room, massive ceiling beams and Spanish arches evoke the bold style of the Cabildo, the seat of colonial government in New Orleans. The neoclassical door surround, the fanlight above the front door, and the millwork within refer to the Federal Style; the wide arches on the rear façade resemble Spanish colonial architecture.

The interiors have a continental French style, injecting a refined, cosmopolitan element. There are a variety of woods in the interior, including finely milled Federal details, painted rough-cut beams, and unpainted heart pine.

The architect's vision was that the house resemble an old West Indian plantation that had grown and changed over time. To create that effect, the two wings that stand alongside the main house look as if they were once freestanding structures. The varying heights and materials of the two wings create the illusion that they may have been built at different times.

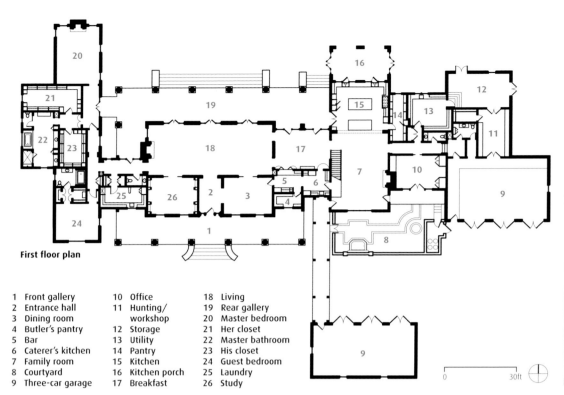

First floor plan

1	Front gallery	10	Office
2	Entrance hall	11	Hunting/
3	Dining room		workshop
4	Butler's pantry	12	Storage
5	Bar	13	Utility
6	Caterer's kitchen	14	Pantry
7	Family room	15	Kitchen
8	Courtyard	16	Kitchen porch
9	Three-car garage	17	Breakfast

18	Living
19	Rear gallery
20	Master bedroom
21	Her closet
22	Master bathroom
23	His closet
24	Guest bedroom
25	Laundry
26	Study

0   30ft

14

Altamira Ranch

Rancho Palos Verdes, California, USA

Marmol Radziner + Associates

Photography: Benny Chan

While impressive in scale, this residence looks and feels as though it emerged from the surrounding environment. This is achieved through the use of building materials that either are or resemble indigenous stone, and an almost 100-percent native California plant palette.

To avoid disturbing the land more than necessary, the four separate buildings—main house, study, guest house, and garage—were cut into the terrain. As a result, the subterranean garage and partially buried main house seem to emerge from the ground as the land slopes toward the ocean.

Carefully located plant massings frame the views of Inspiration Point and Catalina Island and begin to create distinct destinations within the landscape. Curving pathways of decomposed granite gravel were laid out to connect the house with a vegetable garden, olive orchard, camping platform, beach volleyball area, and various look-out points.

Connections to the site extend beyond the physical locations of the structures and outdoor areas to the selection of building and landscape materials that repeat the colors and textures indigenous to the area. Local shale was used to clad the concrete walls, the landscape boulders were harvested from a nearby quarry, and the more than 30,000 plants were contract-grown from native California seed.

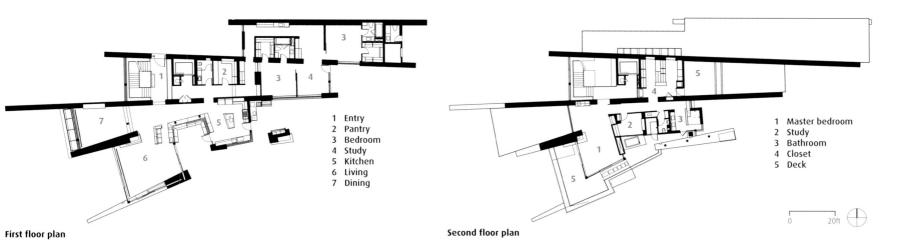

First floor plan

1 Entry
2 Pantry
3 Bedroom
4 Study
5 Kitchen
6 Living
7 Dining

Second floor plan

1 Master bedroom
2 Study
3 Bathroom
4 Closet
5 Deck

0   20ft

Archipelago House

Stockholm Archipelago, Sweden

Tham & Videgård Hansson Arkitekter

Photography: Åke E:son Lindman

The starting point of this design was the direct relationship of the site to the dramatic archipelago landscape; the objective was to offer, within a simple frame, several diverse readings of the space–nature relationship.

The site generated the geometry of the house; it is slipped into the flat surface between two boulders, and turns simultaneously toward the southern sun and western water views. Placing the house on the only flat part of the site avoided any damage to the smooth rocks that characterize the area. The natural ground remains intact, right up to the perimeter of the new building.

The house is conceived as a frame for its surroundings. The smaller rooms are placed at the back, so that the social areas of the house stand out as an open platform criss-crossed by sliding glass. These large, sliding glass planes create a series of outdoor living zones that are sheltered from the strong winds and help to dissolve the limits between interior space, the terrace, and the horizon.

Exterior materials are massive black-stained wood and plywood panels. Interior materials include white oak plank floors, and planed Swedish limestone under the fireplace.

1 Entry
2 Kitchen
3 Living
4 Master bedroom
5 Children's bedroom
6 Bathroom/laundry
7 Studio
8 Guest room
9 Terrace/wooden trellis

0   5m

Floor plan

Asia Modern

Mt Martha, Victoria, Australia

Graham Jones Design

Photography: Chris Groenhout

Located at the highest point of a sloping site, this majestic, resort-styled home captivates its surroundings with views across Port Phillip Bay to the city of Melbourne and beyond.

Being regular travelers to Southeast Asia, the owners loved the feel of contemporary Asian residences—the arrangement of seamless spaces that utilize outdoor living, separate pavilions set among water gardens, and the elegant use of beautiful timbers and natural stone.

Entry to the home is at the rear of the principal pavilion. Passing by a large basement car park, encountering a stone stairway via a trickling water wall,

one looks up into Asian-styled water gardens with timber-planked pathways leading to separate pavilions. A double-volume entry has a wall of glass following the open stair to the upper level. Beyond the imported Javanese stone walls and massive radial-sawn timber screen at the entry are views through the open living room and teppanyaki bar, across the resort pool and "bale" day-bed pavilion, to the tennis court and bay beyond.

The principal kitchen, living room, and master suite are located on the upper level where timber bi-folding doors open up to north-facing stone terraces, protected by huge eaves floating above.

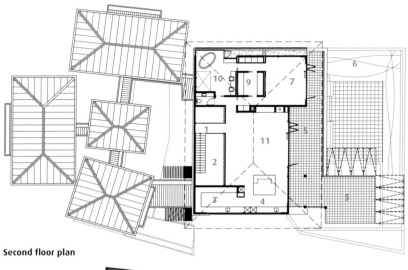

Second floor plan

1 Bridge
2 Void
3 Pantry
4 Kitchen
5 Terrace
6 Pool
7 Master bedroom
8 Stone garden
9 Walk-in closet
10 Ensuite
11 Living

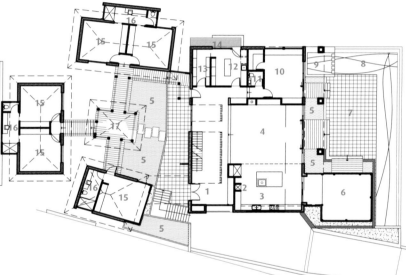

First floor plan

1 Entry
2 Dumb waiter
3 Teppanyaki bar
4 Living
5 Pond
6 Bale daybed pavilion
7 Terrace
8 Pool
9 Spa
10 Study
11 Powder room
12 Laundry
13 Linen
14 Deck
15 Bedroom
16 Ensuite
17 Reading

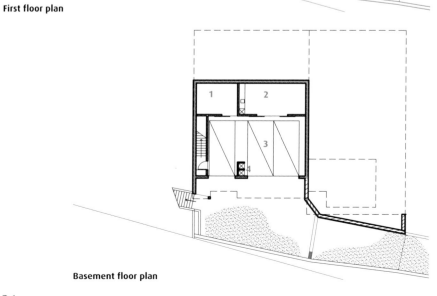

Basement floor plan

1 Storage
2 Gymnasium
3 Garage
4 Dumb waiter

Bach with Two Roofs

Golden Bay, New Zealand

Irving Smith Jack Architects

Photography: Paul McCredie

This home comprising three small buildings and the spaces between sits within a forest clearing overlooking Golden Bay, at the top of the New Zealand's South Island.

Two buildings are inhabited; the larger is for the family, the smaller for friends or children. Peripheral decks connect to the clearing and to sacrificial roofing that protects from the eucalypt trees and collects rainwater. The third building provides independent amenities to the external spaces, which are controlled in volume by the placement of buildings within and to the edge of the clearing, allowing various activities.

The buildings are set back from the sea view to sit within the privacy of the forest, allowing the view to be shared by all from external spaces.

Materials are chosen for their ability to blend into the surrounding bush and dappled forest light, and include oiled cedar, simply finished metals, and eucalypt decking. Interiors are consistent and pure with dark ply wall, ceiling, and joinery linings providing a sense of retreat from the clearing, paralleling the privacy afforded to the clearing by the forest surrounds.

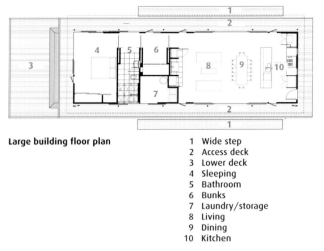

Large building floor plan

1   Wide step
2   Access deck
3   Lower deck
4   Sleeping
5   Bathroom
6   Bunks
7   Laundry/storage
8   Living
9   Dining
10   Kitchen

Small building floor plan

1   Wide step
2   Access deck
3   Guest sleeping
4   Kitchenette
5   Bunks
6   Shower
7   WC

Amenity building floor plan

1   Kayak storage shed
2   Camping workbench
3   Wood store

0   10m

Balmoral House

Brisbane, Queensland, Australia

Arkhefield

Photography: Scott Burrows, Aperture

This house is set on a very steep site facing west within one of Brisbane's middle ring suburbs. The project combines a renovation and new building that reorients the existing house toward its rear.

The existing building becomes a deep, sheltered space encapsulating the private zones of the house. The new house forms the public zone, the fulcrum from which the family distributes its own pattern of interaction. The gap between old and new forms a new gathering place for the house while the back of the existing house becomes the new core. The rear kitchen becomes the center of a new household distribution. The existing house becomes the private living room and new buildings feed its activity.

The yard becomes a captured landscape to the rear, structured for contemplation rather than wilderness. It relates directly to a new public living room, light-filled and sited to take in views to the city over the top of the existing house. The parents' bedroom is perched above, secluded for privacy but engaged through overlooking of the central outdoor space. Parents achieve separation from children at rest while children gain an early domination of living spaces that can alter and grow through adolescence and beyond.

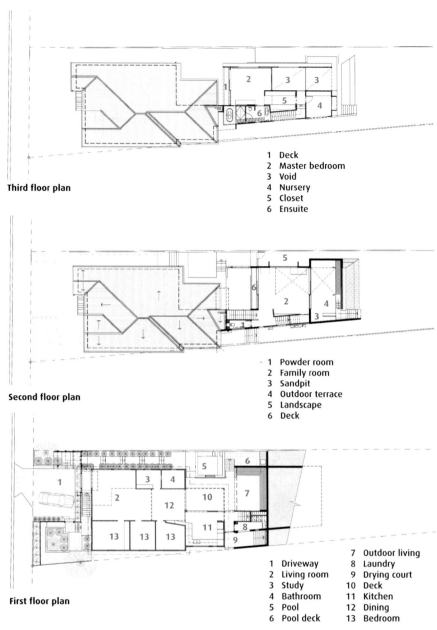

Third floor plan

1 Deck
2 Master bedroom
3 Void
4 Nursery
5 Closet
6 Ensuite

Second floor plan

1 Powder room
2 Family room
3 Sandpit
4 Outdoor terrace
5 Landscape
6 Deck

First floor plan

1 Driveway
2 Living room
3 Study
4 Bathroom
5 Pool
6 Pool deck
7 Outdoor living
8 Laundry
9 Drying court
10 Deck
11 Kitchen
12 Dining
13 Bedroom

Beach House

Upper Michigan, USA

Nagle Hartray Danker Kagan McKay Penney Architects Ltd.

Photography: Scott McDonald – Hedrich Blessing

This 3-acre residential compound tucked into the Michigan sand dunes takes advantage of western lake views as well as vistas up and down the Lake Michigan shoreline. The courtyard to the east is protected from winds at the entry. The 4,000-square-foot main house, with a two-story living room, is the focal point with bedroom quarters to the north, guest room quarters to the south, and a courtyard/garage to the east.

Exterior materials are horizontal and vertical gray weathered cedar siding, slate fireplaces, and fir-framed windows and doors. Sun screens protect the west and south elevations. The decks and roof terraces are variable extensions of the living space. Maple floors, ceilings, and doors and wall trim are selected throughout the interior. Gray slate floor slabs at the entry level have radiant heating. Sun screens, full insulation, and solar glass are some of the sustainable elements.

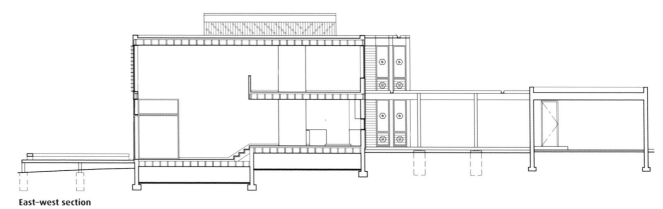

East–west section

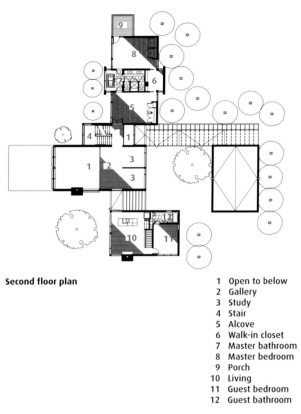

Second floor plan

1 Open to below
2 Gallery
3 Study
4 Stair
5 Alcove
6 Walk-in closet
7 Master bathroom
8 Master bedroom
9 Porch
10 Living
11 Guest bedroom
12 Guest bathroom

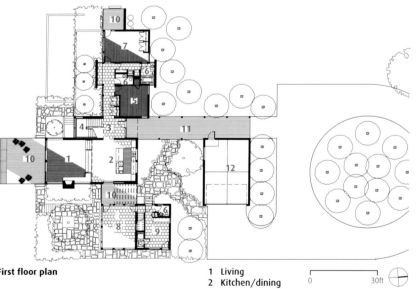

First floor plan

1 Living
2 Kitchen/dining
3 Entry
4 Stair
5 Den
6 Bathroom
7 Bedroom
8 Screened porch
9 Exercise room
10 Deck
11 Covered walkway
12 Garage

0   30ft

Benedict Canyon Residence

Beverly Hills, California, USA

Griffin Enright Architects

Photography: ©Benny Chan/fotoworks

This renovation of a 2,600-square-foot, mid-century hillside house in Los Angeles focused on the roof and the interior public spaces.

A portion of the original gabled roof was replaced with an extended plane of the same angle, resulting in a continuous upwardly sweeping surface. This new roof element was folded up and, after replacing the existing stucco wall with a 50-foot-wide, mullionless wall of glass, the rear façade became a seamless glazed surface that opens up to the existing landscape and pool.

Within the new loft-like space, discrete functional areas are defined through changes in the ceiling plane, placement of furniture, custom built-ins, and lighting. An open shelf with slender steel columns functions as bookcase and room divider.

The ceiling was designed to slope from a height of 7 feet on one side to 11 feet on the other with a plywood panel system housing seemingly randomly placed slots for track light fixtures. This system is punctuated by two light boxes and a skylight, allowing for maximum control and flexibility in the lighting.

Existing tiles were removed from the floor; the concrete underneath was stained and finished with an epoxy resin built up to nearly a half-inch thickness, giving it a liquid quality.

Floor plan

1 Family
2 Living
3 Dining
4 Kitchen
5 Master bedroom
6 Bedroom
7 Bathroom
8 Closet
9 Laundry
10 Garage
11 Pool

Berkshire Residence

Dallas, Texas, USA

Morrison Seifert Murphy

Photography: Charles Smith

The characteristics of this site—its location in a traditional single-family neighborhood, large mature trees in front, and a busy thoroughfare at the rear—shaped the ultimate design of the house.

The U-shaped plan turns its back on the noisy thoroughfare and opens to a courtyard that is shaded by the existing canopy of trees. The mass of the house shields and protects the courtyard from traffic noise beyond. The courtyard is the soul of the house with most of the rooms on the ground level opening directly onto it.

The entry sequence begins with a broken pathway leading past a tall, sentinel-like stucco wall to the front gate of teak set into translucent glass sidelights. Beyond the gate, a covered walkway allows views of the courtyard and the spaces that surround it and leads to a gallery that opens to a display of outdoor sculpture. Finally from the main living space adjacent to the entry gallery, an axial perspective of the courtyard is revealed and the entire concept becomes apparent.

Large sliding doors from the living room and sliding pocket doors from the master suite allow the indoor and outdoor spaces to become one and provide flexible arrangements for daily living and entertaining.

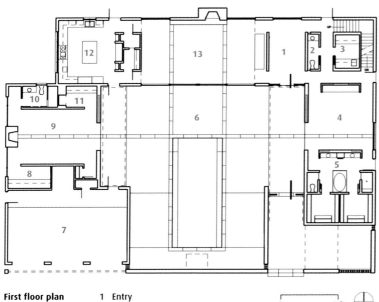

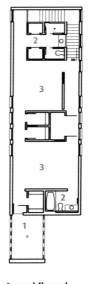

First floor plan

1 Entry
2 Powder room
3 Laundry
4 Master bedroom
5 Master bathroom
6 Courtyard
7 Garage
8 Office
9 Cabana
10 Cabana bathroom
11 Cabana kitchen
12 Kitchen
13 Living

0   16ft

Second floor plan

1 Terrace
2 Bathroom
3 Guest room

Bill's House

Sydney, New South Wales, Australia

Tony Owen Partners

Photography: Brett Boardman

Because the client is a concrete contractor, this house was designed to make maximum use of concrete and solid construction. The brief was to create a unique, iconic home with maximum connections to outdoor spaces.

The house is designed as a series of blocks with different internal levels, which step up progressively from the street. These changes in levels created an opportunity for the strongly stepped external massing as well as the complex interplay of the stairs in the central internal spaces. The L-shaped configuration maximizes the solar aspect for the living spaces. A central courtyard allows light to penetrate the middle of the house and helps to break up the massing of the façade. A feature of the house is the large central staircase, inspired by the James Bond movie, *Never Say Never Again.* The dark polished concrete stair connects the various level change in a single fluid sculptural element.

The curved sail-like rear white walls were designed to reflect the sails of the fishing boats from the Greek Islands. These walls soften the massing and bring a lightness to the house by breaking up the space and progressively dematerializing it into a series of cantilevered vertical and horizontal planes to the rear.

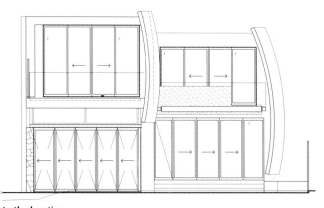

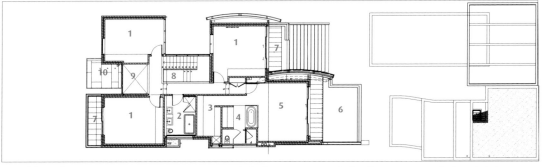

Second floor plan

1	Bedroom	4	Ensuite	8	Open to below
2	Bathroom	5	Master bedroom	9	Void
3	Closet	6	Terrace	10	Roof below
		7	Balcony		

First floor plan

1	Entry	6	Living	12	Terrace
2	Family	7	Lawn	13	Kitchen
3	WC	8	Driveway	14	Courtyard
4	Laundry	9	Storage	15	Study
5	Dining	10	Bathroom	16	Planter
		11	Swimming pool		

Blue Jay Way

Los Angeles, California, USA

McClean Design

Photography: Nick Springett

This house is located on a spectacular lot above Sunset Strip with panoramic views of downtown and west Los Angeles all the way to Santa Monica, the Pacific, and Catalina Island. The design of the house maximizes access to the view, with all the main living spaces looking out over it. The almost 7,000-square-foot house is divided by a water feature and a pool, which became the central design element of the project. It begins adjacent to the driveway as a water wall around which the entry sequence is wrapped. Upon ascending to the main level of the house, the water element becomes an ornamental pool before dropping into the spa below, after which it becomes a 75-foot-long lap pool, the end of which is cantilevered over the slope into the view.

The master bedroom and study are located on one side of the pool, the living areas on the other. Below are several guestrooms, a media room, and a four-car garage. The living room and master bedroom are cantilevered over outdoor spaces and appear to hover against the background of the city below. The palette of materials is soft and contemporary with extensive use of concrete, wood, and stone.

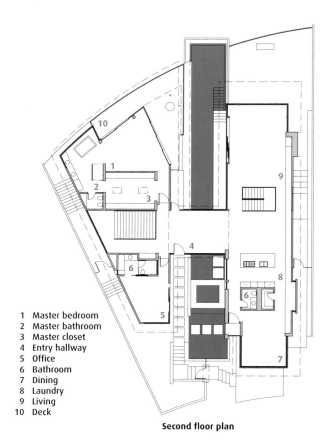

1 Master bedroom
2 Master bathroom
3 Master closet
4 Entry hallway
5 Office
6 Bathroom
7 Dining
8 Laundry
9 Living
10 Deck

Second floor plan

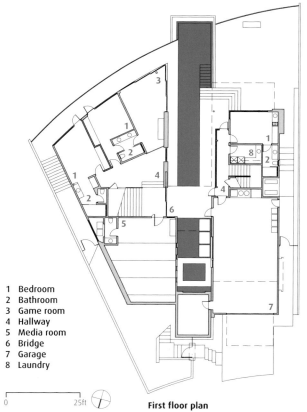

1 Bedroom
2 Bathroom
3 Game room
4 Hallway
5 Media room
6 Bridge
7 Garage
8 Laundry

0   25ft

First floor plan

Box House

Ilhabela, São Paulo, Brazil

Alan Chu & Cristiano Kato

Photography: Djan Chu

The Box House, home of the caretaker of an extensive summer property, is located on Santa Tereza mountain, São Sebastião island, on Brazil's southeast coast.

Because the site is at one of the main entrances to the property, the aim was to create something simple but elegant that could be appreciated by passersby without compromising the caretaker's privacy.

The new building has two floors. A white suspended box contains the bedroom and has magnificent views of the mainland and the São Sebastião Channel. Under the box, at street level, are the living room, kitchen, and bathroom.

The materials were chosen with regard to their availability, cost, and ease of use. Some of the wood used for doors, windows, staircase, shelves, and furniture was left over from materials used to make scaffolding and molds for the reinforced concrete structure.

The 10- by 16-foot white box is supported on one side by an existing retaining wall and on the other by a wall built from local rocks. The other main spaces are the access yard between the box and the retaining wall, the courtyard between the box and the rock, and the void under the box.

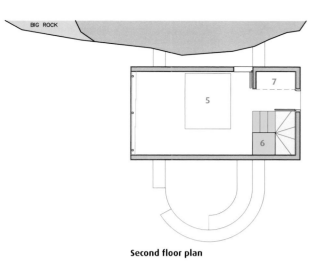

Second floor plan

1 Access yard
2 Courtyard
3 Kitchen and living
4 Bathroom
5 Bedroom
6 TV
7 Closet

0   2m

First floor plan

Brick-Weave House

Chicago, Illinois, USA

Studio Gang Architects

Photography: Steve Hall, Hedrich-Blessing

This house sits on the footprint of a century-old stable in Chicago's West Side. With a modest budget, the owners hoped to salvage the entire building until hidden fire damage was uncovered. Strategically cutting away damage and weaving in new construction allowed 30 percent of the original structure to be reused. The front walls and roof were removed, creating a garden surrounded by a porous "brick-weave" screen.

Variations in ceiling heights and floor levels weave together the two-story garden at the front of the house with the single-story volume at the back through a cascading section.

The brick screen wall demonstrates a sensibility in the use of traditional materials in new and surprising ways. It animates the garden and interior with dappled sunlight, establishing a visual connection to and from the street. Rectangular voids in the screen throw hexagonal patterns of light inside while at night, the pattern reverses: the screen becomes a lantern.

Second floor plan

0   20ft

1	Garden	9	Mechanical
2	Dining	10	Garage
3	Kitchen	11	Family
4	Library	12	Study/bedroom
5	Living	13	Bathroom
6	Powder room	14	Bedroom
7	Laundry		
8	Storage		

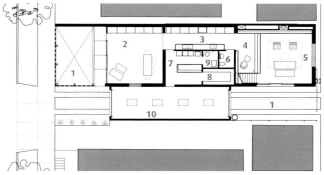

First floor plan

Buisson Residence

Lake Anna, Virginia, USA

Robert M. Gurney, FAIA, Architect

Photography: Paul Warchol Photography and Maxwell MacKenzie Architectural Photographer

Situated on a grass knoll and commanding views of Lake Anna in central Virginia, this house emerges as a long, white painted brick wall with a copper-clad volume cantilevered above the wall.

The entry, living, and sleeping spaces are arranged linearly to maximize lake views and to take advantage of the southern exposure. Large overhangs and motorized shades combine to limit heat gain during the summer while allowing the sun to penetrate deep into the interior during the winter.

The second-floor roof and exterior walls are wrapped in copper with fully glazed east and west walls inset from the ends of the copper volume. The glazed wall at the east end provides abundant light into the double-height entry hall while the glazing on the west end provides light to two bedrooms and views of the lake. A single, large punctuation in the southern copper-clad façade allows views from a second-floor office. The sloping roof and canted front wall are designed to deflect fierce north wind and shed water from intense storms.

Detailing is minimal and precise. The rigor of the design, the linear organization of spaces and the continuous presence of the wall provide a deliberate sharp contrast to the irregular beauty of the landscape beyond.

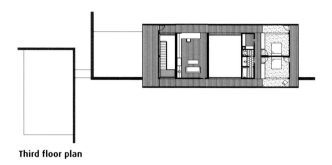

Third floor plan

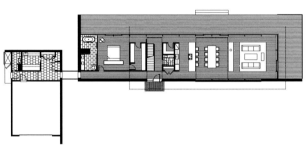

Second floor plan

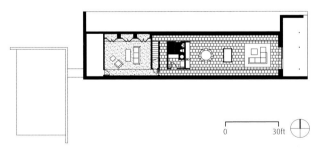

0   30ft

First floor plan

Caroline

Melbourne, Victoria, Australia

Jolson

Photography: Scott Newett Photography

This inner-Melbourne residence is situated on an elevated site on a tight sloping bend in the road with river views to the north.

The architect faced some challenges, including planning restrictions relating to adjoining substations and height covenants, together with a low-profiled street elevation. Views to the river from adjoining properties were also protected by covenant and there were limited opportunities for boundary windows.

The result is a residence sculptured into the site, creating an unexpected volume of interior space, light, and privacy. The house pivots around a central light court and sunken reflection pond that creates a natural cooling device and also bounces light into the lower rooms.

Accommodation includes three bedrooms and a study over two levels. The base palette consists of neutral materials and colors with travertine marble used extensively in the bathrooms, kitchen, and living areas. A bronze sculpture, "Flora Exempla" by Andrew Rogers, was carefully positioned on the surface of the reflection pond.

Detail resolution throughout the house supports continuous internal and external form. Finely mitered stonework, recessed window frames and door tracks, and hidden blinds and services create a seamless integration of indoor and outdoor space and form.

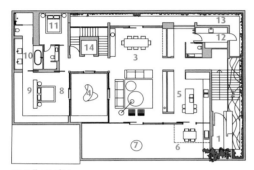

First floor plan

1 First floor entry
2 Stair water feature
3 Lounge/dining
4 Void/sculpture
5 Kitchen
6 Terrace entertaining
7 Outdoor bonfire
8 Master bedroom
9 Dressing
10 Master ensuite
11 Bedroom two
12 Laundry
13 Drying area
14 Lift

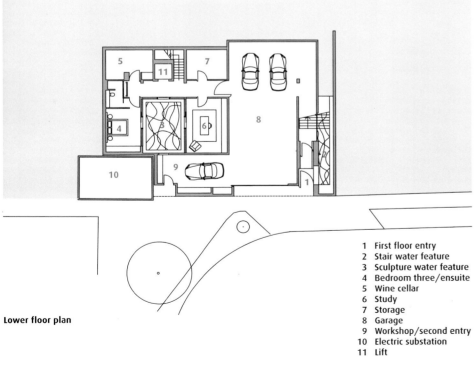

Lower floor plan

1 First floor entry
2 Stair water feature
3 Sculpture water feature
4 Bedroom three/ensuite
5 Wine cellar
6 Study
7 Storage
8 Garage
9 Workshop/second entry
10 Electric substation
11 Lift

0   10m

Casa C

Cuneo, Italy

Damilano Studio Architects

Photography: Andrea Martiradonna

This house was designed to bring the outdoors in by interweaving a sequence of internal and external rooms. The core of the house is the living area, which features two large windows, one with a view to the swimming pool, the other to a more domestic landscape of an external paved area and a meadow beyond.

Comprising ground floor and basement spaces, the house is flooded with light and white absolutely dominates, emphasizing its brightness. The white of the stone is softened by the wood that defines the entrance and the external dining area.

The two sleeping areas occupy the two wings of the house; the master bedroom has its own bathroom, with a shower that breaks through the outer wall with a floor-to-ceiling opal glass wall. In the basement are a small guest apartment, study, and a large gym that includes a relaxation area enclosed in a glass box. These rooms are directly accessible from the outside through terraces and large wooden steps crossing the garden and rising up to the building's entrance level. By night, the lighting plays a spectacular role, accentuating the contrast between the solid and empty elements that characterize the house.

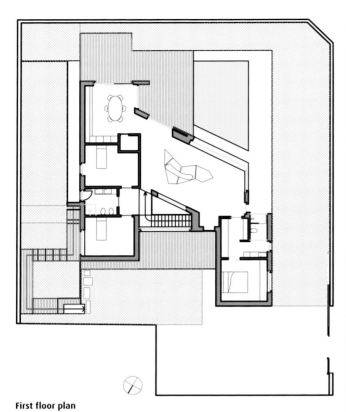

First floor plan

Casa Chihuahua

Chihuahua, Mexico

PRODUCTORA

Photography: Iwan Baan

This house is part of a golf club community in the desert-like northern region of Mexico. The dwelling was designed to accommodate the special climatic characteristics of the area: in winter temperatures can fall to 10 degrees Fahrenheit (–10 °C), while in summer temperatures can rise to above 100 degrees (40 °C). The differences between daytime and nighttime temperatures can vary by as much as 20 degrees. To balance the extreme temperature differences, the house was partially buried in the mountain slope to take advantage of the soil's thermal mass. The colder soil around the house absorbs heat accumulated during the day, and at night the ground gives off heat to the building.

The house is organized around a series of patios and roof openings that provide light, ventilation, and views to different areas of the house. The sloped roof acts as a new topography, which blurs the boundaries between the constructed area and the surrounding landscape.

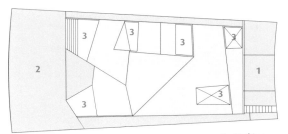

Roof plan

1 Parking
2 Garden
3 Terrace

Entry floor plan

1 Parking
2 Garden
3 Terrace
4 Garage
5 Mechanical
6 Storage
7 Studio

Second floor plan

1 Terrace
2 Hall
3 Circulation
4 Kitchen
5 Staff room
6 Staff bedroom
7 Closet
8 Bathroom
9 Master bedroom
10 Dining room
11 Living room

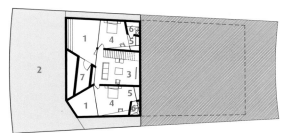

Third floor plan

1 Terrace
2 Garden
3 TV room
4 Bedroom
5 Closet
6 Bathroom
7 Mechanical

0   5m

Casa Fray León

Las Condes, Santiago, Chile

57STUDIO

Photography: Maurizio Angelini

The clients had lived in this neighborhood for almost 30 years, but wanted a larger house. This new 8,600-square-foot residence was designed around the existing trees and landscaping on the site.

The H-shaped plan, with a second level over the central wing, adapts well to the features of the site and creates a number of different patios. The interior spaces are organized around a native tree (*Cryptocarya alba*). Through the hall, an enormous avocado tree is framed toward the north, and a private wing toward the east is delineated by an old macrocarpa cypress. Over the central wing is a second private level with a terrace at one end. On the west wing, the public spaces open toward the northern garden through a porch, and the service areas direct their view toward an ashleaf maple. The services wing extends to the south by means of a roof with an opening that surrounds a native *Crinodendron patagua* that separates the closed garage from the rest of the house. The swimming pool nestles into the site's lowest point, where it relates to the rest of the garden.

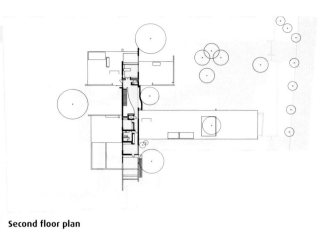

Second floor plan

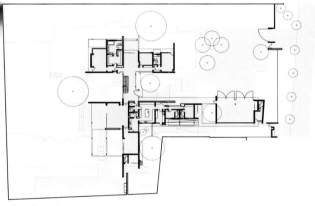

First floor plan

Casa Kübler

Las Brisas de Chicureo, Colina, Chile

57STUDIO

Photography: courtesy 57STUDIO

This 4,520-square-foot house is in a residential park in northern Santiago. The site, mostly surrounded by golf courses and green areas, is characterized by the constant presence of the Andes, high temperatures during the summer, and winds from the south.

The interior spaces of the house are organized around a central patio that is open on the north side to allow views toward the garden. A water mirror runs across a third of its surface, reinforcing this perspective through a porch. The public areas constantly interact with the patio, from the main access to the family room, articulating the service areas toward the west. On the east side, a double-height wall lightly encloses the private area without completely separating it from the patio. The master bedroom opens to a large porch with extensive views over the barbecue area, the swimming pool, and the wider landscape.

Some peripheral walls are extended to direct the views and protect the house from the winds and nearby streets. Slabs extend as oversized eaves to protect windows from the sun and to cover the terraces.

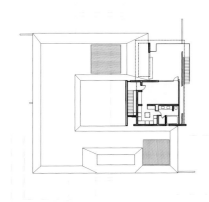

Second floor plan

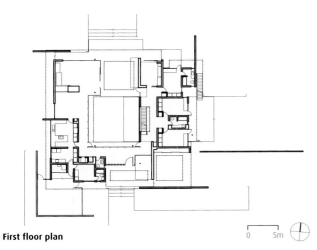

First floor plan

0   5m

Casa Rambed

Barcelona, Spain

Quim Larrea and Katherine Bedwell

Photography: Rafael Vargas

This house, 20 miles northwest of Barcelona, was designed for a young couple with two small daughters. In response to their requirement for comfort, functionality, and transparency, the architects designed fluid spaces that have a continuous relationship with the exterior of the house.

The house is placed on the highest point of the irregularly shaped site; its two wings form a V-shaped plan that engages the house with the surrounding forest. A foyer acts as the hinge of the house from where the two zones are distributed: night/private, and day/public. The kitchen, living room, and dining room are located in the day/public wing. It is a single space, like an "American" family room. The garage/laundry and powder room are also placed in this wing on the ground floor level.

In the night/private wing are the children's bedrooms, a bathroom, a guestroom suite on the ground floor level, and a master bedroom and work studio on the second floor.

Materials were chosen for their ability to integrate well with the surroundings and include limestone, wood, and steel. A color scheme of sober and neutral tones blends seamlessly with the site's natural background setting.

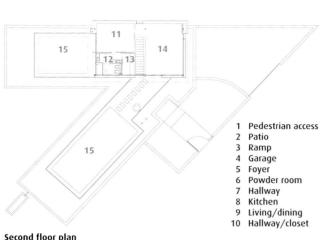

Second floor plan

1	Pedestrian access
2	Patio
3	Ramp
4	Garage
5	Foyer
6	Powder room
7	Hallway
8	Kitchen
9	Living/dining
10	Hallway/closet

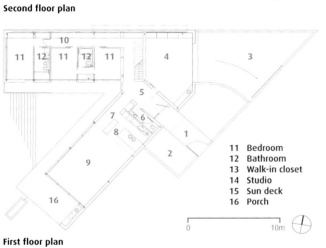

First floor plan

11	Bedroom
12	Bathroom
13	Walk-in closet
14	Studio
15	Sun deck
16	Porch

0   10m

Casablanca

Osaka, Japan

Keizo Matsuda

Photography: Mikio Sugimoto and
Norihiro Matsumoto

Although when construction began on this house there were no immediate neighbors, the architects decided to turn the focus inward, while using as much of the site as possible. The clients' brief included high levels of security and privacy, bright spaces, and a study space that included large bookshelves. Interior parking for a motorcycle was also a requirement.

The house is focused toward the internal private courtyard garden. The entrance is on the same level as the street, to assist with wheeling a motorcycle into the house. Traditional Japanese details include a "doma," (a transitional area between the entrance and the inner part of the house)

and a tatami room. To compensate for the lack of views, the design brings the first and second floors close to the ground floor by means of a void above the ground-floor living area. A 26-foot skylight allows daylight to reach the center of the house. The internal garden courtyard also provides abundant daylight.

On the second floor, the bedroom (equipped as a type of "panic room") and the dining room are reached by separate sets of stairs. High wooden walls surround the internal garden, giving complete privacy.

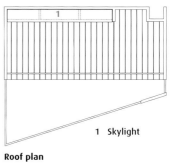

1 Skylight

Roof plan

Second floor plan

1 Bedroom
2 Dining
3 Kitchen
4 Closet
5 Balcony
6 Void

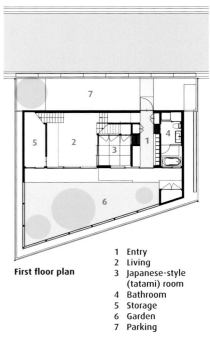

First floor plan

1 Entry
2 Living
3 Japanese-style
   (tatami) room
4 Bathroom
5 Storage
6 Garden
7 Parking

Cascade House

Toronto, Ontario, Canada

Paul Raff Studio

Photography: Ben Rahn/A-Frame Inc.
and Steve Tsai

Set at the apex of a curved street, this house presents as a sculpture of stacked boxes composed from shards of glass and muted black slate. The two-and-a-half-story house is configured in an L shape around an outdoor swimming pool. It has a passive solar design, with most of its energy needs supplied by the sun. The living room, dining room, and a powder room can be closed off from the kitchen and family room at the rear of the house. The children's rooms and a home office are on the second floor, topped by a master suite in a pavilion on the roof.

The most dramatic design strategy is a 13-foot-tall screen of 475 vertically stacked sheets of heavy, jagged-cut glass canted slightly away from the sidewalk. The screen was conceived to maximize sunlight in the living room while providing privacy from the street. Complementing the translucent wall is a freestanding heat-sink wall of dark slate that acts as a central spine. Framing the feature staircase, it rises from the lower level of the house to the top floor, creating a unified visual connection throughout the house. Random apertures provide niches for child play and display, and also dapple the transference of light.

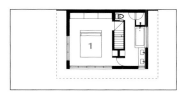

Third floor plan

1 Master suite
2 Bedroom
3 Atrium
4 Study
5 Kitchen/family
6 Dining
7 Entrance vestibule
8 Living
9 Pool
10 Playroom
11 Mechanical
12 Basement suite
13 Garage

Second floor plan

First floor plan

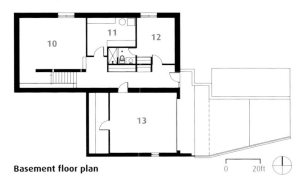

Basement floor plan

0   20ft

Casin di Palazzo Lezze

Venice, Italy

Filippo Caprioglio

Photography: Paolo Monello

This beautiful residence is hidden behind the façade of a 17th-century "palazzo" by Baldassarre Longhena overlooking the Rio della Sensa canal.

The project involved creating a new entrance "hole" in the brick border wall, which leads to the garden through a minimalist corten steel staircase. The main façade was restored conservatively and is now characterized by an internal glass door with steel profiles, painted white, that connects directly to the living area. A library for the owner's 10,000 books covers the full height of the wall on the southwest side of the living area.

The ground floor is a single open living and dining space. Opposite the garden entrance is a typical Venetian water door; access through a new system of steps allows higher access to the house from the water level and protects it from the tides but also allows water to enter underneath the glass box.

A linear stair, made of steel and glass, leads to the upper loft level, constructed of steel, which houses the bedroom and bathroom. The staircase connects to the balcony and to a system of technical steel and glass catwalks, from which the library can be accessed.

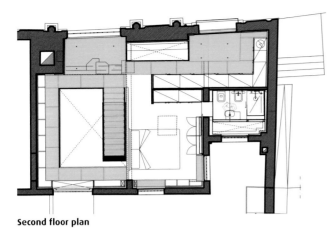

Second floor plan

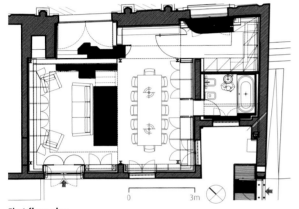

First floor plan

0   3m

Castors House

Tahiti, French Polynesia

Bertrand Portier Architecte

Photography: Tim McKenna

This house was built entirely out of concrete by a small local company. Because access to the site was very difficult, all the concrete had to be transported manually with a wheelbarrow.

The 1,830-square-foot house brings the beauty of its surroundings inside. The double-height living room is an imposing feature of the architecture, from the inside as well as the outside. It offers a magnificent view overlooking the island of Moorea, beautiful sunsets, and a rare panorama. A part of the living room opens directly to the swimming pool, allowing residents to dive directly into the pool. As aluminum-framed windows do not withstand cyclone-force winds if they exceed 8 feet in height, a motorized sectional gate, generally used for hangars and garages, is used to open and close the 16- by 13-foot-wide bay window in the living room.

The living area also features an open fireplace, a seemingly incongruous addition in the hot tropical climate of Tahiti, but the altitude (almost 4,000 feet) means that it can become quite cold during winter.

The house's grey tones help it blend into the natural location. The orange accent color was chosen as an homage to Paul Gauguin, who used it to great effect more than 100 years ago.

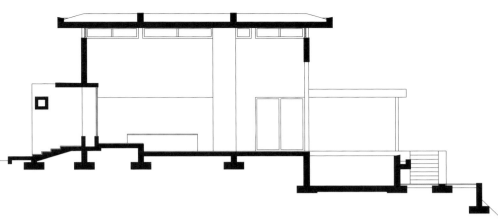

Floor plan

1 Hall
2 Living
3 Kitchen
4 Bathroom
5 Bedroom
6 Terrace
7 Deck
8 Pool

0   4m

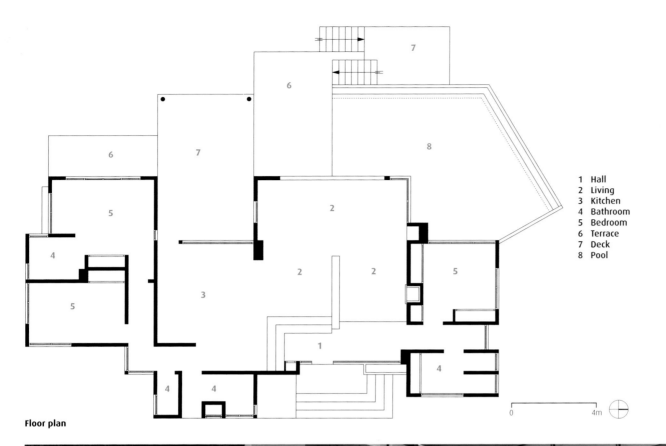

86

Centennial Park House

Sydney, New South Wales, Australia

Innovarchi

Photography: Martin van der Wal

The original cottage on this site was small and dark and did not reflect the grandeur of the surrounding houses in the street. Conceived within a heritage context, this new infill house comprises two separate volumes linked by a double-height space. The footprint of the original house and its main front elevation became the springboard for the site of the first volume that dominates the street elevation. The second volume sits behind and projects beyond the first, creating a double-height entry façade connecting to the existing entry pathway through the English garden which has been preserved. The roof forms mimic the height and pitch of the original house,

and the primary external surface materials are the same as those on the original dwelling.

Strong blade walls running north–south create privacy to and from the neighbors and channel views and solar access throughout the house. Each space in the timber grid is treated with a different timber and glass infill comprising detailing borrowed from buildings in the surrounding neighborhood. This timber treatment is a contemporary reflection of the traditional use of timber joinery in the ornamentation of the brick houses built in the precinct around the time of Federation (1901).

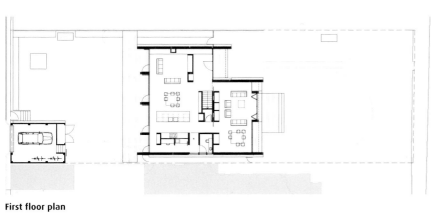

First floor plan

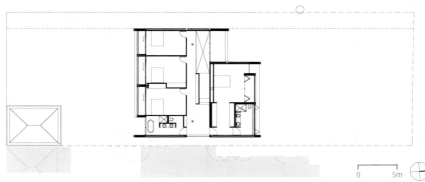

Second floor plan

0   5m

Chestnut Residence

Newport Beach, California, USA

LPA, Inc.

Photography: Costea Photography, Inc.

This house demonstrates that sustainable design is affordable and doesn't have to add cost to any project type, including a custom home.

The two-story, four-bedroom house wraps a central courtyard on three sides with 10-foot-wide pocket doors opening to the outside. The courtyard's climate passively heats and cools the house by taking advantage of the prevailing breezes. The two-story great room is used for night flushing in the summer and a whole-house fan vents the space as required. The house can be open or closed depending on the climate conditions, allowing the occupants to shape their living environment. Private spaces are located upstairs and are connected by a perforated plywood "bridge" that allows the movement of light and air. The translucent skylight, with significant insulation properties, lights the kitchen area of the great room, which is closed to mitigate traffic noise from the adjacent highway.

As a demonstration of passive and active systems, a 5.3 kW photovoltaic panel system integrated with the cool roof provides much of the home's energy needs. The green features were made affordable by the trade-offs in the simple palette of materials used on the house: integral color plaster (no painting), Douglas fir siding, and drywall throughout the interiors.

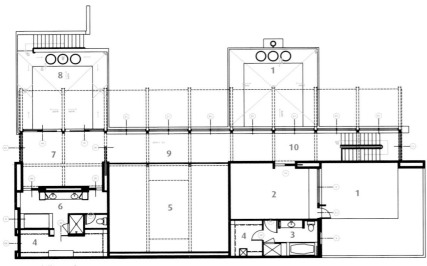

Second floor plan

1	Roof	6	Master bathroom
2	Bedroom	7	Master bedroom
3	Bathroom	8	Sunset terrace
4	Wardrobe	9	Bridge
5	Open to below	10	Hall

First floor plan

1	Entry	9	Powder room
2	Garage	10	Workout/guest room
3	Laundry	11	Guest room
4	Pantry	12	Guest bathroom
5	Kitchen	13	Pool bathroom
6	Great room	14	Library
7	Storage	15	Dining
8	Game room		

0   20ft

Chimney House

São Paulo, Brazil

Marcio Kogan + Studio MK27

Photography: Reinaldo Coser

A wooden patio with trees, formed by the volumetry of the house and a concrete wall, articulates the entire program of this São Paulo house. The living room is enclosed in the boxed ground floor and wide windows open it to the external space. This room, just 21 by 34 feet, with a ceiling height of less than 7 feet, is a cozy space, accentuated by the textured concrete ceiling made with narrow wooden formwork.

The two-story volume, arranged perpendicular to the living room, contains the service program, the kitchen, and a TV room on the ground floor and three bedrooms on the second floor. Sliding wooden brise soleils filter the light into the interior and the windows open out to the patio. The master bedroom extends outward to a wood-decked solarium. In this space a ground fire can be used to cook a barbecue on a sunny day or to light the house on a dark night. The chimneys on the rooftop are of varied shapes, inspired by the chimneys on the rows of houses in the city of São Paulo.

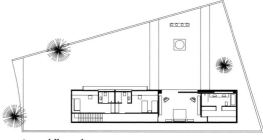

Second floor plan

0 ———————— 10ft ⊕

First floor plan

Colonial House

The Bahamas

Robert Adam Architects

Photography: Scott Frances and Tim Aylen

This house, part of a seaside development in The Bahamas, sits on a dune crest. Designed in a Colonial style, it features traditional Caribbean details and provides more than 10,000 square feet of accommodation.

Upon entering the house through the front door, the spectacular view of the sea is immediately revealed. The main accommodation is contained in the central section of the house, arranged around a double-height stair hall. Two subsidiary wings contain a library and play room, away from the more public areas of the building. A wide portico on the entrance front terminates a vista from the approach road and the seaward façade. A full-length two-story portico overlooks the pool and the ocean.

Interiors by Monique Gibson.

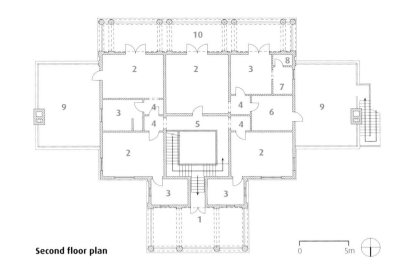

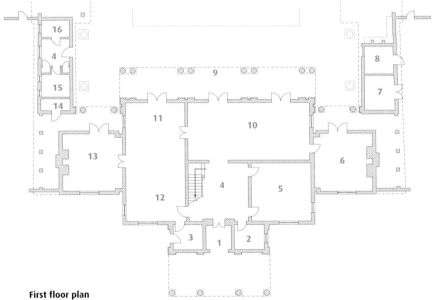

Second floor plan

0   5m

1 Portico
2 Bedroom
3 Bathroom
4 Lobby
5 Landing
6 Dressing
7 Shower
8 WC
9 Balcony
10 Veranda

First floor plan

1 Lobby
2 WC/cloaks
3 Utility
4 Hall
5 Dining
6 Library
7 Storage
8 Plant
9 Veranda
10 Drawing room
11 Informal dining
12 Kitchen
13 Family
14 Wine cellar
15 WC
16 Shower

Concrete House

Mar Azul, Villa Gesell Department, Buenos Aires Province, Argentina

BAK Arquitectos

Photography: Daniela Mac Adden

Mar Azul is a seaside town 250 miles south of Buenos Aires, characterized by its large dune beach and leafy coniferous forest. This low-budget house in the forest was designed to have minimum impact on the landscape, to be low-maintenance, and to be constructed as quickly as possible. To accommodate the site's 20-foot incline, the house is half-buried so that it merges into the site, presenting a different façade on each side. The southwest façade is buried in the sand and features a continuous glazed opening. The northwest curtain wall façade features a balcony that allows distant views while a series of concrete partition walls protect the privacy of the occupants.

The house does not have a main entrance. In this forest microclimate, orientation was not important since the pines provide protection from the sun and wind. Car parking, the barbecue, the sunbathing platform, and other outdoor features were not organized by functional reasons but rather by the topography. The garden was left largely untouched, to retain the natural quality of the landscape.

Furniture, designed by the architects, is made from Canadian pine recovered from automotive packing, providing a connection to the forest surrounds. The table is a concrete slab joined to the exterior wall.

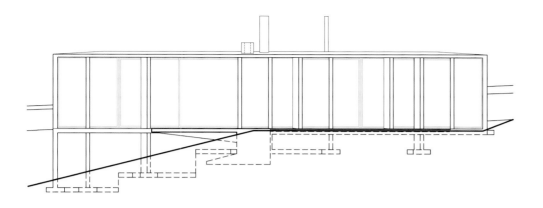

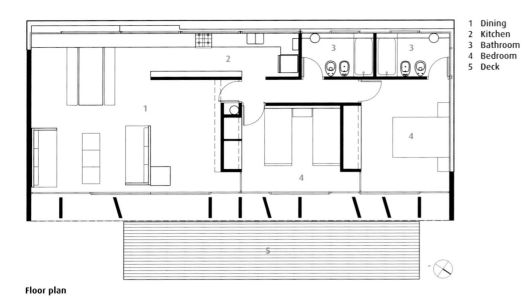

Floor plan

1 Dining
2 Kitchen
3 Bathroom
4 Bedroom
5 Deck

Coogee Beach House

Sydney, New South Wales, Australia

Lexis Design and CM Hairis Architects

Photography: Thomas Bloch

This new family residence in Sydney's eastern suburbs overlooks Wedding Cake Island. A linear and sculptural envelope, the emphasis is on maximized natural light, effective sightlines—including ocean views—and exceptionally livable space.

The spatial volume is tailored to the contours of the landscape, and is articulated with seamless, fluent lines. The internal planning connects spaces and living areas with comfortable fluidity. The volume sequence, with double-height cut-outs, split levels, and half-height walls, promotes internal and external sightlines and is linked by a dynamic floating staircase.

Tonal veneers, white glass, Caesar stone, and aluminum were selected for the spacious kitchen; veneered walls and pivot doors add further continuity and introduce warm tones to the area. Warmth and visual interest are also integrated through the discerning use of Calcutta marble and connecting travertine floors.

Specialist finishes on key surfaces were selected to offset the building's clean lines with contrast and texture. Raw, unrefined materials alongside honed and polished stone, and ink-stained timber floors bring depth and sensory interest. Intimacy is further introduced in the upper levels by the use of soft wool carpeted floors to mute acoustics and add tactility to the private areas of the house.

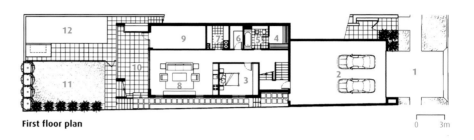

First floor plan

1 Driveway	7 Laundry
2 Garage	8 Rumpus
3 Bedroom	9 Water tanks
4 Sauna	10 Patio
5 Bathroom	11 Garden
6 Linen	12 Pool

0   3m

Third floor plan

1 Balcony
2 Study
3 Bedroom
4 Closet
5 Ensuite
6 Bathroom
7 Void

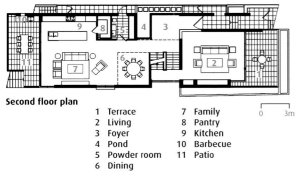

Second floor plan

1	Terrace	7	Family
2	Living	8	Pantry
3	Foyer	9	Kitchen
4	Pond	10	Barbecue
5	Powder room	11	Patio
6	Dining		

0   3m

Crans-près-Céligny Houses

Geneva, Switzerland

Group8

Photography: David Gagnebin-de-Bons and Benoît Pointet

Crans-près-Céligny is a peaceful village located at Lake Geneva, about 9 miles from the city of Geneva. These houses are part of a residential development in an almost agricultural environment with views toward the Alps.

The site is between the railway and the lakeside. The architects describe the three separate red volumes as "stones thrown in a grass field," which form a single entity through their interaction. The complex sculptural volumes offer ever-changing perceptions of the project; deformation and perforation are used to respond to the site, avoiding repetitious symmetry.

An essential part of the project is its "materiality." Ochre-colored concrete was chosen to give the ensemble an unusual and tactile texture and a strong silhouette against the green lawn site.

Second floor plan

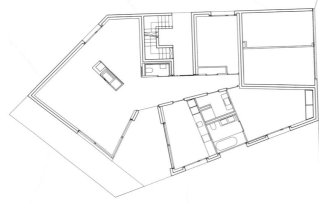

First floor plan

Davidson Residence

Laguna Beach, California, USA

McClean Design

Photography: Sven Etzelsberger

This new house replaces an existing house that the clients had occupied for several years. Not wanting to move from their current location, they desired a house that would relate primarily to its garden with an open, contemporary feel.

The site is on a suburban cul-de-sac close to a beautiful beach but views to the ocean are limited and available from the second level only. In addition, the size of the upper level was severely restricted by local view preservation requirements. With this in mind, all the primary rooms are located at ground level, including the master bedroom.

The main living space includes a 30-foot retractable glass wall that allows the kitchen and living room to feel like part of the garden on warm days.

The kitchen island extends into the backyard and the garden and living spaces flow seamlessly when the doors are retracted.

The curved front of the house is finished in dark metal panels, contrasting with the horizontal lines of the rest of the house. The double-height entry links the two levels of the home and focuses the view to the rear yard and fountain.

The sleek palette of materials includes black metal panels, stainless steel, aluminum, glass, charcoal cabinets, and stone.

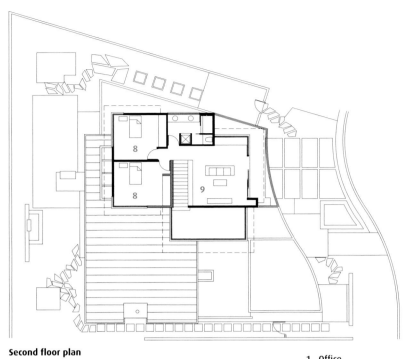

Second floor plan

1 Office
2 Garage
3 Kitchen
4 Entry
5 Master bedroom
6 Master bathroom
7 Living
8 Bedroom
9 Family

First floor plan

0   20ft

Downing Residence

Tucson, Arizona, USA

Ibarra Rosano Design Architects

Photography: Bill Timmerman

Barely discernable from its mountainside backdrop, this 3,500-square-foot house pivots to follow the topography and optimize views toward city lights and nearby and distant mountains. The three carefully nestled split-face block pavilions are built as independent structures linked by glass circulation spaces that blend with surrounding rock outcroppings.

The house opens to cross ventilation to maintain comfort passively and efficiently. The southeast-facing windows collect warmth in the winter while west-facing glass is kept to a minimum.

While the house's material palette is simple—block, steel, glass, birch, and mesquite—the result is dramatic and uplifting spaces with a spatial complexity resulting from the ever-changing daylight, seasonal blooms, dramatic storms, and desert sunsets.

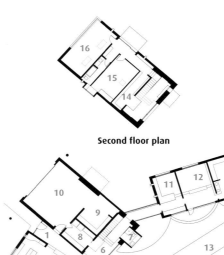

Second floor plan

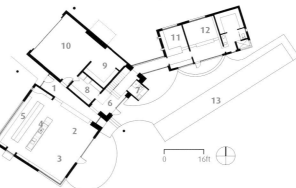

1 Entry
2 Living
3 Dining
4 Kitchen
5 Pantry
6 Gallery
7 Powder room
8 Laundry
9 Workshop
10 Garage
11 Study
12 Master bedroom
13 Lap pool
14 Library
15 Guest bedroom
16 Weaving studio

0   16ft

First floor plan

Edge House

Kolbotn, Norway

Jarmund/Vigsnæs AS Architects MNAL

Photography: Ivan Brodey and
Nils Petter Dale

The Edge House is located at Kolbotn, a suburb south of Oslo. The clients, a young couple, asked for a spectacular house on a limited budget. They had purchased a challenging site with a 25-foot height difference from the access road to a plateau, and they wanted a house that "looked like you could shoot a James Bond movie in it."

To preserve the plateau, the building was pushed toward the eastern perimeter of the site, suspended above the slope on slender steel columns. The entrance stair rises along the slope through the house up to the plateau.

This strategy avoided costly excavation, hiding the technical connections in the stair. At the same time it preserved the existing characteristics of the site, creating a dramatic interplay between volume and site. The entrance condition and the experience from the inside attempts to underline this interplay.

The compact interior is horizontally organized, with bedrooms and bathrooms effectively along a corridor.

The main structure is steel, with a polished concrete floor slab. The interior is clad in birch plywood, the exterior in naturally colored fiber cement board.

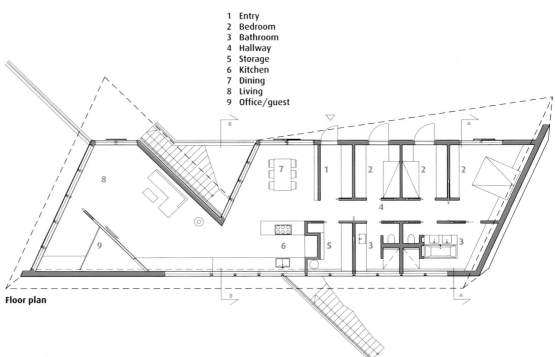

1 Entry
2 Bedroom
3 Bathroom
4 Hallway
5 Storage
6 Kitchen
7 Dining
8 Living
9 Office/guest

Floor plan

Elysium

Noosa, Queensland, Australia

Arkhefield

Photography: Scott Burrows, Aperture

This house, part of the exclusive Elysium community, was designed with the aim of combining the attractions of coastal living with regionally inspired sub-tropical modernism and the qualities and natural assets of the specific site.

The concept centers on strong simple forms and materials that create volume, light, shadow, and define space. Three simple forms hang off a "living spine," creating a transparent, dynamic circulation and gallery space. Each element contains a different function and is defined by its own material. Junctions between these forms are special but unpredictable spaces of tense high volumes of filtered and colored light. The spaces flow out to the edge of the property and the integration of indoor to outdoor space is seamless.

The pool is designed to integrate with the dining area, creating colored, warm reflected light inside the space. The living and kitchen functions wrap around the outdoor living area, which cantilevers out into the park to the north. The elevations are deliberately ambiguous and dynamic as they change from walls to screens within the same material and surface.

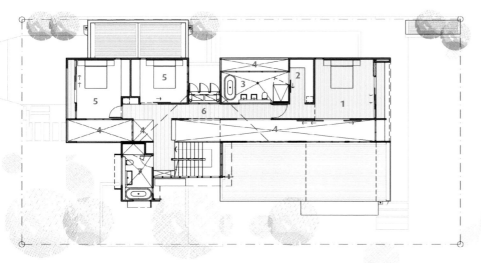

Second floor plan

1 Master bedroom
2 Walk-in closet
3 Ensuite
4 Void
5 Bedroom
6 Gallery
7 Bathroom

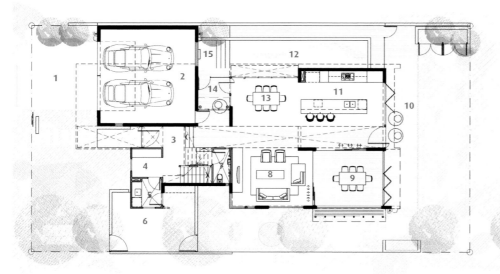

First floor plan

1	Driveway	9	Outdoor living
2	Garage	10	Deck
3	Lobby	11	Kitchen
4	Study	12	Pool
5	Laundry	13	Dining
6	Drying court	14	Courtyard
7	WC	15	Spa
8	Living		

Enclosed Open House

Singapore

Wallflower Architecture + Design

Photography: Albert Lim

The owner's desire for a spacious home resulted in the development of a program that internalizes spaces such as pools and gardens normally regarded as exterior features.

The intermingling of internal gardens and column-free vistas on the ground floor produces a continuous and unbroken visual depth that ties together the entrance foyer, swimming pool, formal living area, internal garden court, and formal dining areas.

The environmental transparencies at ground level and between courtyards are important in passively cooling the house. All the courtyards have differing material finishes and therefore differing heat gain and latency

(water, grass, granite). As long as there are temperature differences between courtyards, the living, dining, and pool house become conduits for breezes that move between the courtyards, similar to the way land and sea breezes are generated.

Thick masonry walls on either side of the house minimize temperature fluctuations inside and also act as "ducting" to guide air currents between courtyards. At the second story, adjustable solid hardwood louvers allow the desired amount of breeze and sunlight to filter through. Substantial trellising on the ground floor minimizes sun entry into habitable areas.

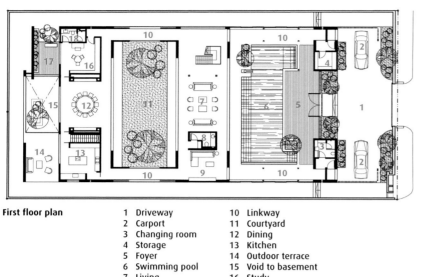

First floor plan

1	Driveway	10	Linkway
2	Carport	11	Courtyard
3	Changing room	12	Dining
4	Storage	13	Kitchen
5	Foyer	14	Outdoor terrace
6	Swimming pool	15	Void to basement
7	Living	16	Study
8	Powder room	17	Outdoor deck
9	TV area	18	Bathroom

Second floor plan

1	Flat roof	7	Linkway
2	Void to	8	Void to courtyard
	swimming pool	9	Bedroom
3	Study	10	Bathroom
4	Master bedroom	11	Family
5	Closet	12	Outdoor balcony
6	Master bathroom	13	Void

0   4m

Farm House

Toten, Norway

Jarmund/Vigsnæs AS Architects MNAL

Photography: Nils Petter Dale

The clients inherited an abandoned farm overlooking Lake Mjøsa. The existing barn was demolished due to rotting foundations, but the cladding, despite being more than 100 years old, was in good condition and was used in the construction of this new 1,600-square-foot house. The spatial complexity, exposed construction, and material simplicity of the barn also inspired and informed the new architecture.

The interior organization has a dual focus, opening the entire façade toward the lake to the north, while stepping the central space down to the terrace at the west side of the house. The series of common spaces at these sloping axes are visually connected, opening the full length of the house. A children's loft is above; the parents' part of the house is below.

The main section rises toward the south to allow for the low winter sun to enter the building. The glazed and lofty winter garden works as a heat collector during winter, and as a heat buffer for the rest of the house during summer.

The principal construction material is wood; the windows are lined with aluminum, and the ground floor is exposed concrete.

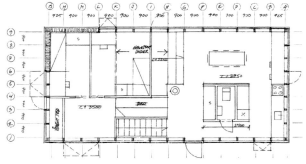

Second floor plan

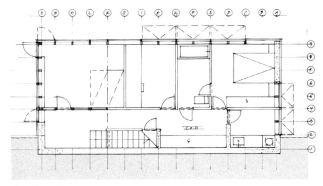

First floor plan

Fennell Residence

Portland, Oregon, USA

Robert Oshatz Architect

Photography: Cameron Neilson

Approaching this house from a dock on the Willamette River, the sweep of curved glue-laminated beams and the rich hue of exposed wood and copper trim make it stand out from its neighbors.

Inspired by its setting, the house was designed as a series of curves that seem to flow over one another. A glu-lam beam dives into the floor at a side courtyard, while another breaks high overhead. Beyond the entry to the house and around a staircase is a great open living space with a full wall of glass looking out to the river and shoreline beyond.

The home is filled with natural light that seems to roll down under the curved ceiling and exposed beams before spilling into the living space. Gaps in the structure are filled with glass, making the building feel light and transparent, with subtle reflections that imply depth. Clerestory windows open to allow natural ventilation.

By contrast, the plan of the house is rectilinear, tight, and logical. The client enjoys loft-style living and there are few interior partitions, with the master suite looking over the main living space, sharing the view.

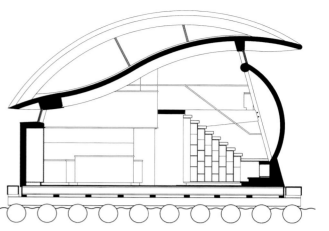
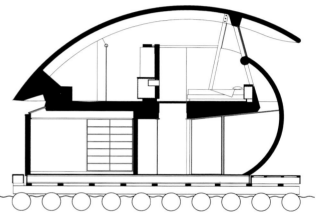

127

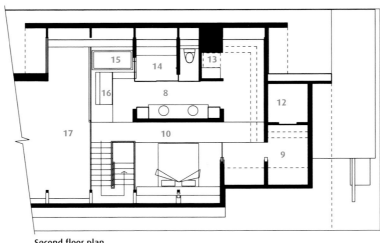

1 Living
2 Dining
3 Kitchen
4 Wine cellar
5 Office
6 Guest room
7 Deck
8 Bathroom
9 Closet
10 Master bedroom
11 Entry
12 Bulk storage
13 Laundry
14 Shower
15 Bathtub
16 Seat
17 Open to below

Second floor plan

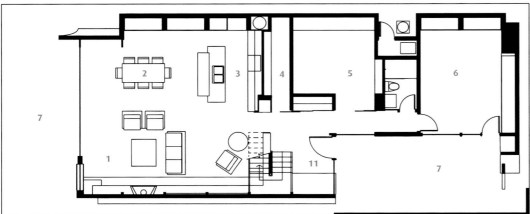

First floor plan

0   5m

Flamarion

San Pedro Garza García, Nuevo Leon, Mexico

RDLP Arquitectos

Photography: Arq. Jorge Taboada

The built environment of San Pedro Garza García, a city in Nuevo Leon state in Mexico, has reached its limit and there are geographic barriers to further growth. The city therefore encourages reutilization and remodeling of old houses. This residence, situated close to one of Garza García's main streets was remodeled using the existing structure.

The existing structure was unfortunately quite disproportionate, making it difficult to take advantage of the existing spaces. The solution was to partially demolish the front of the house in order to generate a "veranda" to control pedestrian and vehicular access. This veranda was designed so that the house's main entrance still had a presence from the street.

Inside the house, the new layout located the social and service areas on the first floor and the family area on the second floor. The social and family areas are connected by double-height areas, but can be separated by a sliding wall. In the backyard, the pool and patio are integrated into the building by means of a swimming lane that runs alongside the house and is enhanced by a water fountain on each side.

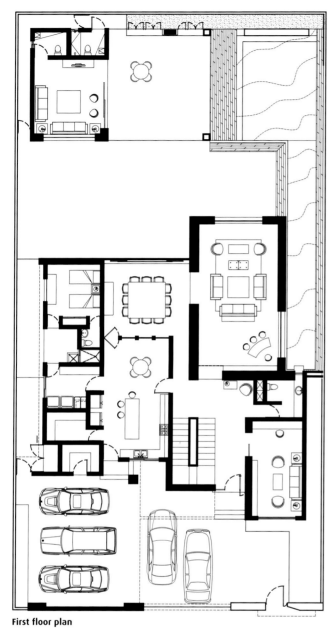

First floor plan

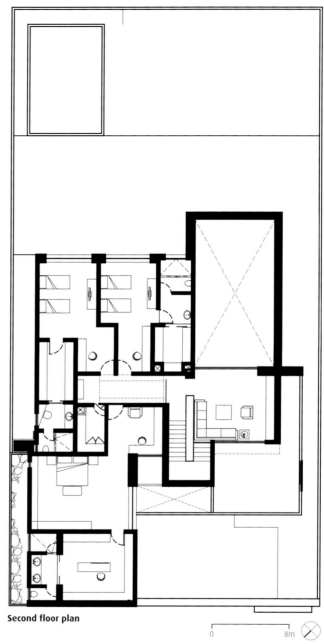

Second floor plan

0 ——————— 8m

Foote-Pelletier Residence

Bremen, Maine, USA

Barba + Wheelock

Photography: Sandy Agrafiotis

This house is situated on a 13-acre rural lakeside property with no directly abutting neighbors. Over the past 30 years, the owner has developed the compound, adding a salvaged 19th-century carriage barn, converting a boathouse, and enlarging the original teahouse. This main house is the latest in the collection.

The program includes a two-story central hall with living, dining, and kitchen, and a guest loft above. Flanking this central hall are two smaller wings, each with a bedroom and bathroom. The wings have dramatically differing characters: one is modern and glass-filled, while the other is traditional.

Each of the main architectural elements is situated on one of the two main axes, forming a cross. The classically proportioned form of the exterior reflects the distinct objectives of the two owners, celebrating them carefully at each gable end. The modern gable of the west wing is fully glazed from base through pediment; the traditional gable of the east wing presents a Palladian window and solid pediment; the gable at the south-facing kitchen has a traditional base, culminating in a fully glazed pediment; finally, the formal entrance façade is dominated by a Vitruvian-proportion colonnade with 24-inch diameter Tuscan order columns.

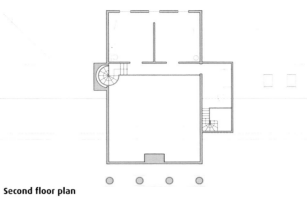

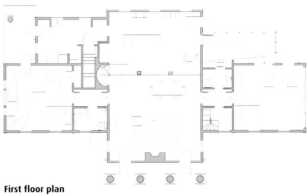

135

Fort Ward Bunker House

Bainbridge Island, Washington, USA

Eggleston Farkas Architects

Photography: Jim Van Gundy

The site for this family residence is a hilltop occupied by a decommissioned military bunker—the fire control station for Gunnery Nash at Fort Ward at the south end of Bainbridge Island. The purchase price of the property was set based on the assumption that substantial costs would be incurred removing the circa-1904 bunker to allow for construction of a new residence.

Rather than battle the bunker, an alliance was made. A concrete garage is aligned with the bunker, and together they serve as the base of the house. The primary living spaces are placed on a steel frame above. Within the house, 24-inch-deep storage zones flank the living spaces. The kitchen, stair, and service areas form a core within the open plan. An open stair connects to the bedroom floor above. A slot along the floor of the upper landing links the two floors spatially while offering the children a lookout over the kitchen and living room.

Since the house was completed, the owners have been working to restore the native vegetation, which has been returning since the army abandoned the site. Meanwhile, the bunker—hunkered in below—is restored not for coastal defense, but as the world's coolest play fort.

Third floor plan

1 Master bedroom
2 Master bathroom
3 Office
4 His dressing
5 Her dressing
6 Laundry
7 Bedroom

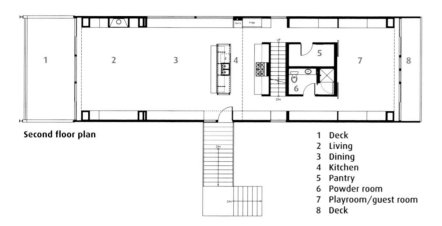

Second floor plan

1 Deck
2 Living
3 Dining
4 Kitchen
5 Pantry
6 Powder room
7 Playroom/guest room
8 Deck

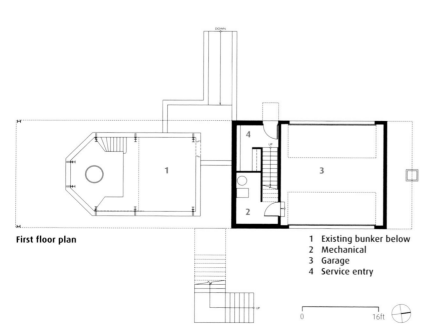

First floor plan

1 Existing bunker below
2 Mechanical
3 Garage
4 Service entry

0   16ft

Forty-five Faber Park

Singapore

ONG&ONG Pte Ltd

Photography: Derek Swalwell and
Tim Nolan

The priority in the design for this house was to maximize outdoor play space for the clients' young children. The living spaces were to be open to the outdoors, with a clean, contemporary aesthetic.

The residence is separated into three main elements. The top, more private element is cantilevered over the driveway. The titanium and zinc cantilever gives the entrance to the house an enclosed, protected feel. The ground floor accommodates the social areas and features sliding pocket doors that open directly onto the lower garden. An organic, sculptural staircase acts as an anchor point for the house and a hinge for the two perpendicular main

elements. The third element of the house is the naturally lit basement, vertically connected to the social spaces of the house. One light source for the basement is the void garden, the other a window that looks into the swimming pool.

The house features numerous sustainable design elements including orientation to provide maximum cross-ventilation of the social spaces, the use of in situ concrete and terrazzo to provide thermal mass, the use of locally sourced teak, strategic positioning of skylights to provide ventilation and lighting, and recessed windows to provide shade and reduce solar gain.

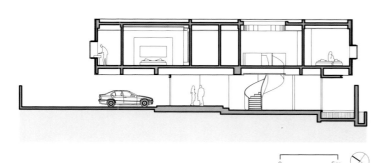

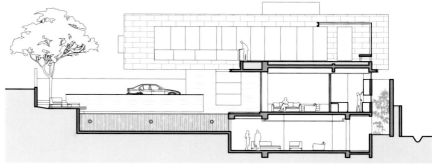

0   5m

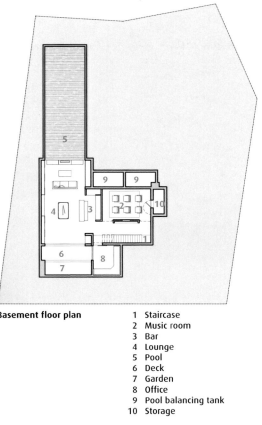

Basement floor plan

1 Staircase
2 Music room
3 Bar
4 Lounge
5 Pool
6 Deck
7 Garden
8 Office
9 Pool balancing tank
10 Storage

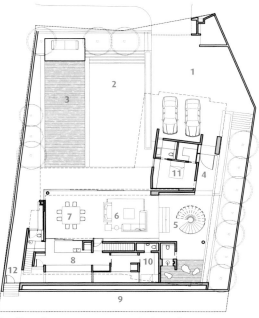

First floor plan

1 Car park
2 Garden
3 Pool
4 Entry
5 Hall
6 Living
7 Dining
8 Kitchen
9 Yard
10 Service room
11 Guest bedroom
12 Rear entrance

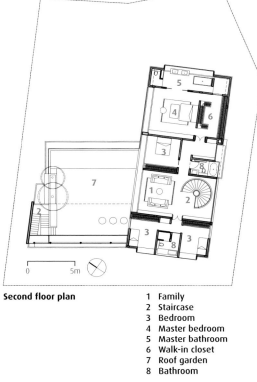

Second floor plan

1 Family
2 Staircase
3 Bedroom
4 Master bedroom
5 Master bathroom
6 Walk-in closet
7 Roof garden
8 Bathroom

143

Frisina Residence

Montecito, California, USA

The Warner Group Architects, Inc.

Photography: Eric Figge

This 5,400-square-foot exposed steel and glass residence is firmly rooted on a challenging 2:1 sloping hillside in Montecito, California. Both stories utilize dramatic, floor-to-ceiling 12-foot glass walls for full views of the Montecito foothills and the Santa Barbara coastline.

The front elevation features exposed steel moment frames around both garage doors and the first-floor living room/second-floor master suite volume to let the homeowners literally live among the 50-foot eucalyptus trees.

The steel beams and columns allow the cantilevered steel and glass canopy to protect the 12-foot corner glass wall of the living room below.

The steeply sloping site allowed for a private, living backyard with a 16-foot waterfall flowing down the rear retaining wall, which is screened with Italian cypress. Throughout the first floor, honed black granite flooring flows from interior to exterior so that the living space appears to double when the stacking glass pocket doors are fully hidden away.

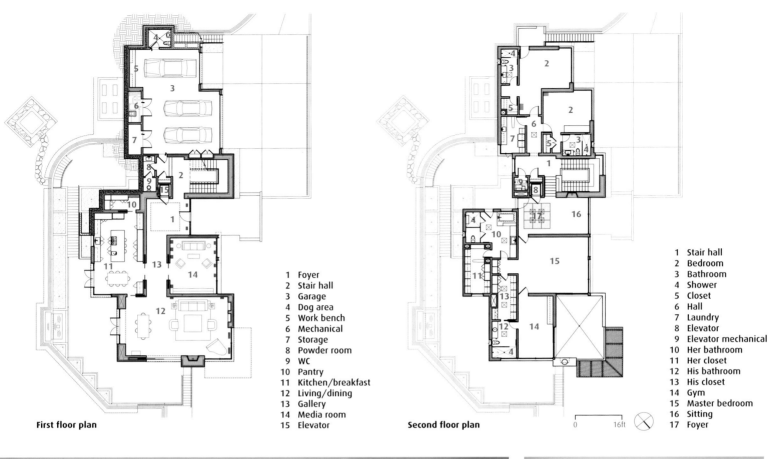

First floor plan

1 Foyer
2 Stair hall
3 Garage
4 Dog area
5 Work bench
6 Mechanical
7 Storage
8 Powder room
9 WC
10 Pantry
11 Kitchen/breakfast
12 Living/dining
13 Gallery
14 Media room
15 Elevator

Second floor plan

0   16ft

1 Stair hall
2 Bedroom
3 Bathroom
4 Shower
5 Closet
6 Hall
7 Laundry
8 Elevator
9 Elevator mechanical
10 Her bathroom
11 Her closet
12 His bathroom
13 His closet
14 Gym
15 Master bedroom
16 Sitting
17 Foyer

Glade House

Lake Forest, Illinois, USA

Frederick Phillips and Associates

Photography: Barbara Karant/Karant + Associates Inc.

In this historic district, where large traditional houses prevail, this house seeks a return to simple agrarian forms, colors, and textures typical to the region, but lost long ago.

Two distinct gable structures recall, loosely, a farmhouse "T" plan, but their exact configuration is atypical. Door and window openings are proportioned and spaced with classical regularity, while a continuous band of clerestory windows separates volumes, lightens structure, and adds dimension to certain interior spaces. The prevalence of natural light precludes the need for artificial light during daylight hours, and openings that respond to prevailing breezes substantially reduce the need for air conditioning.

The simple rectangular plan maximizes the efficiency of the building envelope. The driveway segments the lower level at the main entrance and leads to a turn-around adjacent to the garage. The resultant reduction in ground floor area minimizes the footprint (1,285 square feet) in a landscape originally designed by Frederick Law Olmstead.

Detailed with jewel-like precision, the ordinary is given richness without superfluous decoration. The roof is zinc-coated copper, horizontal rain screen siding is clear Western red cedar, and shingles are Grade A Eastern white cedar. Heating is in-floor hydronic set in Gyp-Crete under rift-sawn white oak.

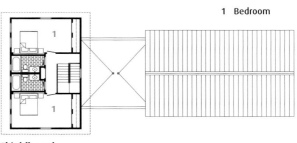

Third floor plan

1 Bedroom

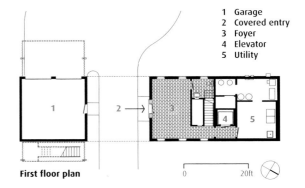

Second floor plan

1 Kitchen
2 Dining/living
3 Elevator
4 Master bedroom

First floor plan

1 Garage
2 Covered entry
3 Foyer
4 Elevator
5 Utility

0   20ft

149

Gradman House

Inverness Park, California, USA

Swatt | Miers Architects

Photography: Cesar Rubio

This small country residence is located on a steep up-sloping lot in Inverness Park, California, near Point Reyes National Seashore. The site contains large mature oak, fir, and bay trees and has beautiful filtered views of Tomales Bay to the northwest and wetlands to the northeast.

The goals of the project are common to West Coast residential living—promoting enjoyment of the outdoors, maximizing views, and sensitively knitting the house to the land. The house and access road are carefully situated to protect as many existing trees as possible. The house is designed with five floor levels, which gently step with the topography and create distinct zones for living. The entry and circulation space, located at the middle level, is designed as a light-infused central spine and joins the "public" living and dining spaces at the lower level with "private" bedroom areas at the upper levels. Each bedroom opens to its own private hillside garden at the top of the site, while the living and dining areas open to expansive terraces with magnificent views to the bay and wetlands below.

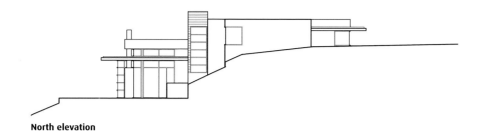

North elevation

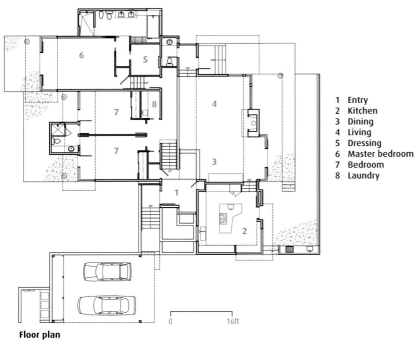

Floor plan

1 Entry
2 Kitchen
3 Dining
4 Living
5 Dressing
6 Master bedroom
7 Bedroom
8 Laundry

0   16ft

Grangegorman

Dublin, Ireland

ODOS Architects

Photography: Ros Kavanagh and
Barbara Corsico

This new house is an alternative to more traditional city-center infill projects; an unapologetic piece of architecture sitting within a strong urban context defined by site and planning constraints. The building is essentially two living plates over a workshop, connected by a vertical service and circulation core. It has been designed to sit discreetly within its more traditional context, while giving the end of the terrace an appropriately strong presence.

The building is entered under a canopy, which extends internally to create a "suppressed" area inside the front door, emphasizing a triple-height stairwell beyond. The experience of this space is further enhanced through the introduction of a full-width rooflight running the length of the building, flooding this volume with natural light. Accommodation comprises a second-floor open-plan living, dining, and kitchen space linked to the first-floor bedrooms and bathroom by the triple-height circulation zone. This circulation volume extends down to the ground floor, providing access to the lower garage area, the walled back garden behind, and the paved front garden facing the street. The enclosed back garden, to the rear of the property, is seen as a landscaped courtyard that opens directly into the ground-floor volume and is partially sheltered by the cantilevered structure above.

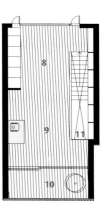

Third floor plan

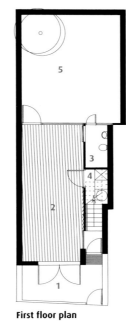

1 Front garden
2 Garage/study
3 Bathroom
4 Store
5 Courtyard
6 Bedroom
7 Ensuite
8 Kitchen/dining
9 Living
10 Terrace
11 Void

First floor plan

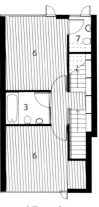

Second floor plan

0   5m

Grid House

Serra da Mantiqueira, São Paulo, Brazil

Forte, Gimenes & Marcondes Ferraz
Arquitetos

Photography: Ale Schneider

This project involved three main issues: the demand for a single-story house, the wish to establish a direct relationship with the land and nature, and the need to provide privacy for all family members. The site is a small valley, protected from the wind and close to a lush native forest.

The basis of the design is a wooden modular grid, supported by sets of concrete pillars and large trussed corten steel beams, creating a light and ethereal structure. The area's high humidity led the designers to raise the house above the ground. A mix of closed and open modules highlight the structural continuity and enhance the spaces through which the garden can be seen.

The residential block contains a bathing area, a social area, a guest room and the owner's apartment, and three separate modules, with two bedrooms each, for the children.

The leisure pavilion, located at the top of a hill, with generous mountain views, is divided into two blocks, with the same modulation as the main residence. A further three service pavilions, housing a garage, housekeeper's house, staff accommodation, dressing rooms, and warehouses, use the same basic module in a stone structure.

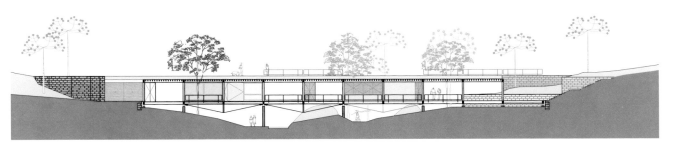

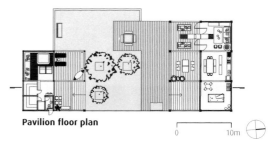

Pavilion floor plan

0   10m

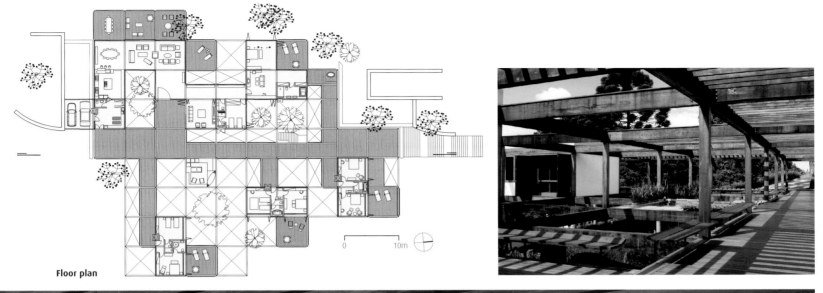

Floor plan

0   10m

159

Gwinganna

Queensland, Australia

Paul Uhlmann Architects

Photography: Remco Photography

This house, designed for a couple and their three small children, is in a small coastal beach community on Australia's east coast. The site affords long southern views down the local river system, while the yard has views north over the local village. The house was planned around this northern outdoor space, which incorporates a covered terrace/dining area.

The L-shaped plan protects the external areas from the prevailing cold southerly breezes, while opening up to the cooling summer breezes from the north. The terrace area has a sliding door and screen system that retracts completely into a wall cavity. The bedroom wing is situated half a level above this main living area, and provides shading from the hot westerly afternoon sun. The wing has a series of louver windows within the building plan and external screening to allow cross ventilation through this area.

A laundry deck is included on the upper level to provide easy access for the family. The lower level accommodates the vehicle storage, study, and rumpus room for the children. These areas also have views along to the river over the adjoining parkland. An adjustable aluminum louver system has been incorporated to provide privacy from the parkland below.

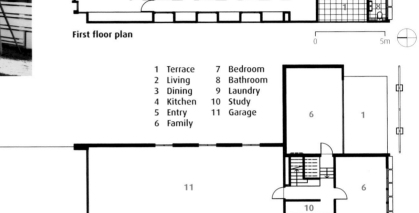

First floor plan

0 ____ 5m

1 Terrace   7 Bedroom
2 Living   8 Bathroom
3 Dining   9 Laundry
4 Kitchen   10 Study
5 Entry   11 Garage
6 Family

Lower floor plan

Harbour Residence

Sydney, New South Wales, Australia

Marchese + Partners International

Photography: Andrea Francolini

The brief for this house on Sydney Harbour was for a timeless modern residence, suitable for both day-to-day living and, on occasion, hosting large family gatherings. The clients also wanted a special master bedroom retreat, separate from the rest of the house.

The design was based on a horizontal platform upon which all the main living areas are located. The main living, dining, and kitchen spaces at the rear of the residence enjoy unobstructed views of Sydney Harbour and the Gladesville Bridge. Floating above this platform, a dynamic folded white plane encapsulates the four children's bedrooms. The master suite was conceptualized as a separate silver box that sits atop the white plane separated from the main house.

The plan is simple and elegant. A light well located on the central axis assists in admitting winter sun into the core of the home. A sculptural staircase animates this central circulation axis. A minimalist palette of finishes is used throughout the residence. Gray terrazzo tiled floors clad the main living platform, walls are white, and joinery is in American walnut and white polyurethane paint. This is offset by the charcoal stacked slate wall that anchors the northern edge of the home.

Second floor plan

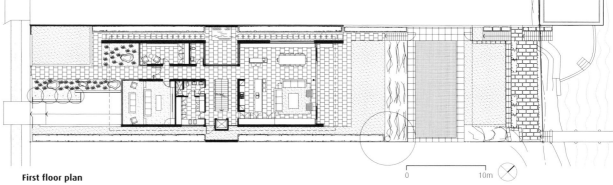

First floor plan

0   10m

163

Hidden House

Los Angeles, California, USA

Standard

Photography: ©Benny Chan/fotoworks

Accessed only via a half-mile unpaved road, this 7-acre site offers expansive views of the city but at the same time seems a world away from Los Angeles. An existing two-bedroom house was kept substantially intact while the architects designed an entirely new home around the original space.

Today, the original two-bedroom cottage is incorporated into the house as the living and dining room. A new kitchen, family room, office, garage, master bedroom suite, and children's bedroom were added, essentially doubling the volume of the house to 3,500 square feet. The new house is arranged around two main courtyards. The main living spaces open up onto the interior courtyard, while the exterior courtyard looks out over the city in the distance. The self-contained cubes are arranged around the original footprint in such a way that they make order of the disorder.

The house also features several sustainable materials and features, ranging from the redwood cladding, to reclaimed end grain block wood, to the cork flooring in the office, and highly efficient appliances/equipment. Excellent cross ventilation and daylighting reduce the need to run air conditioning or heating or energy-consuming electrical lighting. The house is insulated with sustainable cotton and is solar-ready.

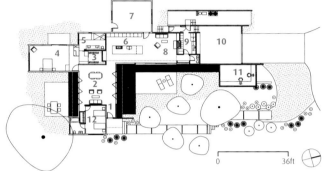

Floor plan

1	Entry	7	Playroom
2	Living/dining	8	Family
3	Master closet	9	Laundry
4	Master bedroom	10	Garage
5	Master bathroom	11	Office
6	Kitchen	12	Guest room

Hong Kong Villa

Hong Kong, China

Olson Kundig Architects

Photography: Benjamin Benschneider

Overlooking the South China Sea in Shek-O, an historic fishing village in the southeast corner of Hong Kong Island, this house is designed to face the elements and bring in the stunning coastal scenery. The design includes large expanses of glass revealing dramatic views in every direction; seamless transitions from inside to outside merge the house into its landscape, while broad overhangs provide protection from the tropical sun and driving rains.

On the uphill side of the house, the formal entry is accessed via a large central courtyard that incorporates a reflecting pool. Flanking that dramatic central entry space are the more intimate portions of the house—the living

and dining areas—with private quarters book-ending the single-level plan. A second pool runs along the ocean side of the house, visually merging with the water and island-studded coastline in the distance.

Inspired by traditional Chinese architecture and furniture, the house uses a simple palette of materials—concrete, steel, stone, and glass—relying on exacting detail and craftsmanship to provide the visual counterpoint. Artist Mary Ann Peters painted a full-length wall mural in the gallery that crosses the central axis.

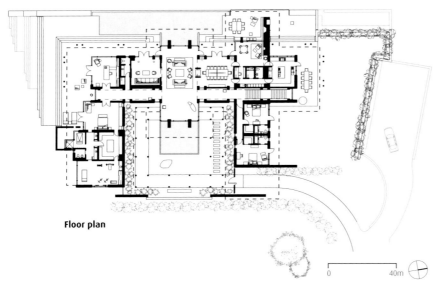

Floor plan

0   40m

Horizontal Space

Cuneo, Italy

Damilano Studio Architects

Photography: Andrea Martiradonna

This house is a horizontal composition of pure volumes of constant height and rectangular shapes. A set of wide steps, flanked by a feature pomegranate tree, leads to the entrance and into a series of consecutive spaces accessed by a large central hall.

The four bedrooms and four bathrooms are arranged around the central living room. This open-plan area features large windows and sliding doors that open up to views of the garden and countryside beyond. A covered deck with deep overhangs provides shelter from the sun and the weather.

Teak floors in the living room extend throughout the house, promoting a warm environment; a stone feature wall creates a sculptural effect that complements the bold furniture.

The kitchen is characterized by a large horizontal slot above the work bench, which frames the neighboring houses and mountain views. In the master suite, a translucent sliding door separates the bathroom from the bedroom. The plainer rear façade features a balcony and a separate entrance to the basement spaces, which comprise a gym, garage, and service spaces.

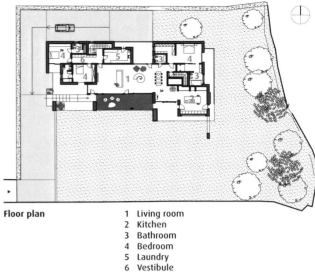

Floor plan

1 Living room
2 Kitchen
3 Bathroom
4 Bedroom
5 Laundry
6 Vestibule

House 2 for a Photographer

Casas de Alcanar, Tarragona, Spain

Carlos Ferrater, OAB

Photography: Alejo Bague

This house is on a long and narrow site (820 feet long by 60 feet wide) that is perpendicular to the sea at the Ebro Delta in Tarragona. A stand of 60 Washingtonian palm trees planted between the beach and house reflects the primarily agricultural nature of the area.

The house, set far back from the water and built on a platform 2 feet above the flood-prone terrain, is a rich, sculptural composition of three irregularly shaped one-room pavilions that surround a central exterior living area. The three pavilions comprise a living-dining-kitchen area, a master bedroom, and an artist's studio with a sleeping alcove for guests. An exterior stair at the back of the studio leads up to a lookout and solarium on the roof.

The tall, white masonry planes of the three pavilions cast deep shadows and direct sunlight and breezes into the central area and into the house. The large, glazed openings of the rooms direct views and offer a series of alternative glimpses through the house. Doors opening onto the central area are deeply recessed, providing sun protection and additional spaces inside the perimeter walls. Ceiling heights of up to 16 feet add a sense of grandeur to the otherwise modest size of the rooms.

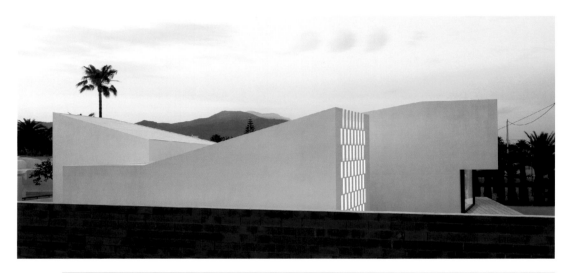

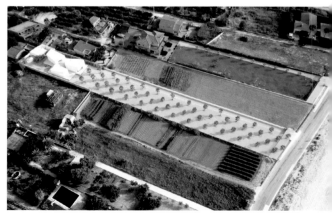

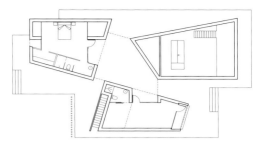

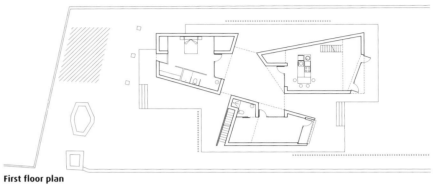

House 53

São Paulo, Brazil

Marcio Kogan + Studio MK27

Photography: Rômulo Fialdini

The volume of this house is a product of the São Paulo building regulations and the site's peculiar shape, which is about 33 feet at the front and almost 100 feet deep. The building code permits a two-story building to be built right up to the site's side limits. A third floor is allowed as long as the lateral setbacks are respected.

The house was conceived as a monolithic wood and mortar block with another concrete and glass volume upon it. Because of the site's small frontage and volume, it was important to admit as much light as possible into the interior, hence the large windows.

The house's top volume, which comprises the living room on the first floor and the bedrooms on the second floor, is a glass box with wooden sunshades that open as folding doors. The front and back façades were designed to be completely closed or opened.

From the outside, when the sun screens are closed, the openings are difficult to distinguish, with all the wooden surfaces making up a pure single volume.

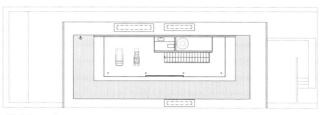

Third floor plan

Second floor plan

First floor plan

House D

Ljubljana, Slovenia

Bevk Perovic Arhitekti

Photography: Miran Kambic

Although the client brief for the house was simple—one living room, one bedroom, and a gymnasium—the task was difficult because of the relatively small site. To compensate, a large part of the house was hidden below grade, forming an introverted world secluded from the surroundings.

The underground area contains workout/fitness space, a sauna and swimming pool, a music room, and three atriums. It forms a vast base for the house, covering almost the entire site.

The living room with reception area, open kitchen, and dining area is on the first floor and continues over the external terraces. Planted atriums, which appear as small gardens, offer glimpses of the world below.

On the upper floor, a bedroom with ensuite continues onto a terrace the same size as the room. This terrace offers a broad view of the city and the neighborhood.

The concrete structure enabled vast spans and spaces. The concrete was cast on site, sanded, and polished, revealing the sedimentary character of the material. The house's exterior appearance is enigmatic, entirely different from other houses in the neighbourhood. The closed cubic forms with a street façade made of polished concrete reveal nothing of the luxurious world inside.

Second floor plan

First floor plan

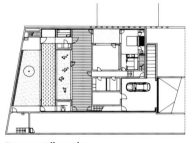

Basement floor plan

0   12m

House Dijk

**Blauwestad, Groningen,
The Netherlands**

JagerJanssen architecten BNA

Photography: SAPh/Rob de Jong

This house is in the new housing development of Blauwestad, where 1,500 new houses are planned around a man-made lake. The owners wanted a large house that would also feel spacious. Three floors were required: one for parking cars and motorbikes, a ground floor with kitchen and living, and a further level with four bedrooms.

A continuous skin of anthracite-colored corrugated sheets clads the building. Continuing from the roof to the façades, the cladding acts as a "raincoat" for the house, and protection from the bleak easterly winds. From the interior, viewing axes over the Groningen landscape optimize the spatial experience. The kitchen is in the center of the ground floor and defines an axis perpendicular to the house. From here the parents can keep an eye on their children playing in the garden.

The difficulty with this design was the basement, which had to remain above ground-water level. This restriction, together with a maximum building height dictated by the master plan, determined the division and position of the three floors. The basement is approximately 5 feet below ground level, the first floor 3 feet above. By lifting the entire volume and placing it on the slightly contracted basement, the house appears to hover above the ground.

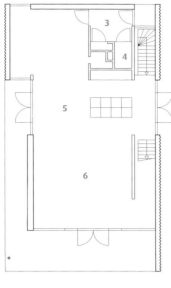

Basement floor plan

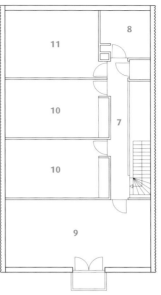

First floor plan

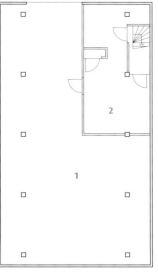

Second floor plan

1	Basement	7 Vestibule/void
2	Scullery	8 Bathroom
3	Entry	9 Master bedroom
4	WC	10 Bedroom
5	Kitchen	11 Study
6	Living	

0 — 5m

House G

Lake Constance, Germany

K_M Architektur

Photography: Nadja Athanasiou

This unique family home, with spectacular views over beautiful Lake Constance, merges with the elements, using concrete, glass, and wood as structural materials. Wood predominates, forming the external skin, but also acting as a primary construction material.

A loggia encircles the building on the water side, fulfilling the owners' wish for open living spaces. All spaces are focused on the view. A courtyard with glass on all sides separates the two living rooms without obstructing the view. The loggia connects all the water-side rooms and creates a flowing transition between interior and exterior. Floor-to-ceiling glass doors and frameless windows intensify the effect.

The outer skin of cedar wood encloses the diverse openings and views and visually unites the building, despite its interplay of open and interior spaces. A combination of geothermal heating and rooftop solar panels produce most of the energy for the home, supplemented by a stove in the living room.

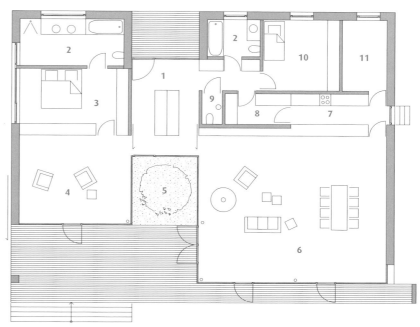

Floor plan

1	Entry	5	Atrium	9	WC
2	Bathroom	6	Living/dining	10	Guest room
3	Bedroom	7	Kitchen	11	Mechanical
4	Library	8	Storage		

House HanenDick

Eelde, The Netherlands

JagerJanssen architecten BNA

Photography: Rob 't Hart

The clients had a number of requests for this new house on one of the oldest streets in Eelde. Existing old trees were to remain untouched while the free-standing building was to accommodate bicycle storage (but no garage), a separate room for piano lessons, separate formal and informal entrances, and at least four bedrooms.

Preserving the character of the village street was a priority, as was linking the house to the footprint of the original farmhouse that formerly occupied the site, and preserving views of a small medieval church nearby.

The result is a brick volume, penetrated by a box that seems to have fallen into the main mass. The brick house is kept pure and abstract by continuing the bricks onto the roof; gutters are subtracted from the brick mass and sealed by a metal lattice. Braided masonry is used for the transition from ascending to sloping brickwork on the roof.

The brick volumes house service functions, bicycle storage, and the piano room. The rectangular box contains all the living spaces. The two bedrooms to the garden side share a balcony and there are several opportunities for intriguing vistas, including a view of the church spire from the master bathroom.

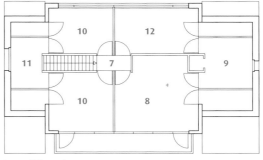

Second floor plan

10		12
11	7	9
10		8

1 Entry
2 Closet/WC
3 Living
4 Kitchen
5 Scullery
6 Bicycle shelter
7 Vestibule
8 Master bedroom
9 Master bathroom
10 Bedroom
11 Bathroom
12 Study

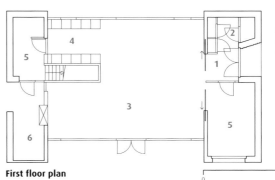

First floor plan

0   5m

185

House HB

Pirnice, Ljubljana, Slovenia

Bevk Perovic Arhitekti

Photography: Miran Kambic

House HB is an attempt to define a new kind of domestic environment in a neighborhood of typical post-war two-story houses. It recalls the form of traditional houses—low and elongated rural buildings more associated with stables than habitation. Its site, at the top of a small hill, is a typical Slovenian suburban setting—close to the city but rural at the same time.

Despite its dominant position, the house seems to merge with the landscape. The roof and side façades are clad in 20-foot-long aluminum plates, which merge the surfaces together into a clean, anonymous shape. It retains the iconographic features of a traditional house, such as a pitched roof, relatively small volume, and linear spatial sequences.

An entire floor of the house, containing the bedrooms and library, is "submerged" into the hill underneath it, while the living areas are located in the upper part of the house. The two elevations offer quite different living experiences: the lower structure is built in concrete and is oriented toward the hidden patio; the upper structure is made of glass, entirely transparent along the longer edges of the building. The open interior is organized by the selection of furniture, grouped to form "virtual" rooms.

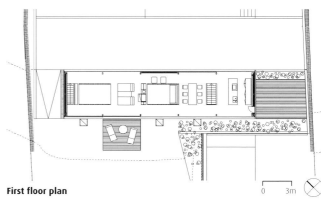

First floor plan

0   3m

House in Curitiba

Curitiba, Brazil

Una Arquitetos

Photography: Nelson Kon and
Victor Fernandes

This house was planned around a number of towering araucaria trees that existed on the site, providing character to an otherwise unremarkable urban plot. The clients, a philosopher couple with two children, included in the program a library that they specified should be independent, though easily accessible from anywhere in the house.

The site's downward slope suggested locating the house on the higher level. The longitudinal volume of the 3,400-square-foot house was used to define two different external aspects: one that interacts with the araucarias,

which were left intact; and on the opposite side, a constructed garden connected to daily activities.

A central double-height space, with a balcony and dining room, divides the house into two blocks. A further two balconies at the top floor reveal views over the nearby araucaria forest.

The entry and vehicle parking are at basement level. A guest bedroom opens to the courtyard and the front of the site.

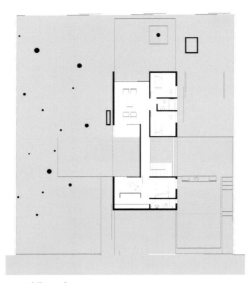

Second floor plan

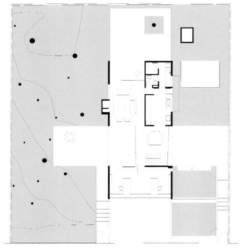

First floor plan

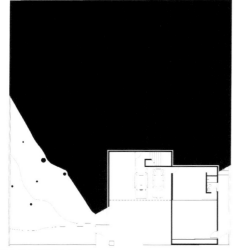

Basement floor plan

House in Kakinokizaka

Meguro, Tokyo, Japan

Satoshi Okada

Photography: Nacasa & Partners, Shinkenchiku-Sha

This house is located in one of the most prestigious residential areas in Tokyo. The client had three major requirements: off-road parking for six cars (including four "supercars" in a purpose-built gallery); a high-ceilinged living room; and a reinforced concrete structure with an exposed concrete finish, similar to a fortification. This both protects the residents' privacy and provides rigidity and fireproofing in the event of an earthquake.

The floor plan is quite simple. The main entrance is placed between the supercar gallery and the garage for ordinary vehicles. The north–south axis that starts at the entrance becomes a linear circulation core, to which every

room is attached. A "patio" functions as a medium between the supercar gallery and the family living quarters. Set-back regulations limit the building height to less than 22 feet; thus the master bedroom beneath the living room was set a half-story down below ground level to allow a higher ceiling in the living room and views to the supercar gallery over the patio from the main bedroom and from the living room.

The façade is articulated both horizontally and vertically, to provide respite from the otherwise featureless concrete walls, and to provide some context with the neighboring houses.

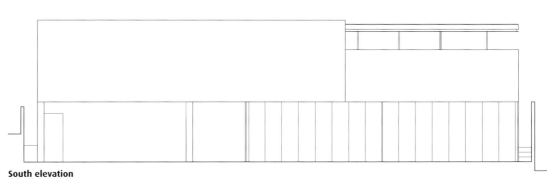

South elevation

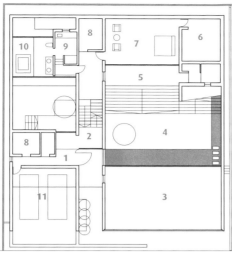

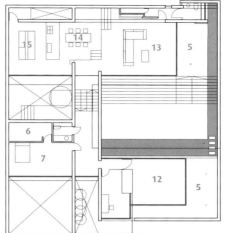

1 Entry
2 Hall
3 Gallery
4 Garden
5 Terrace
6 Closet
7 Bedroom
8 Storage
9 Utility
10 Bathroom
11 Garage
12 Guest room
13 Living
14 Dining
15 Kitchen

Basement/first floor plan

First/second floor plan

House in Las Casuarinas

Lima, Peru

Javier Artadi

Photography: Alexander Kornhuber

This house is a strong, minimalist composition, built on a steeply sloping site with commanding views over the city of Lima. The complex program includes traditional components such as living room, dining room, and bedrooms, and additional spaces including a gym, sauna, studio, and a small apartment.

To accommodate the various parts of the program, the architects proposed a series of "boxes": three volumes perpendicular to each other. One box contains the vertical circulation; another, parallel to the street, contains bedrooms and a family room. The third box, which contains the living room, has a dramatic cantilever at the front of the house. The remaining parts of the program are arranged along a back wall and in two small secondary volumes.

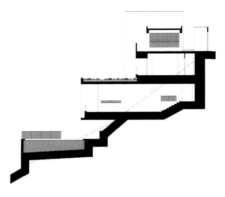

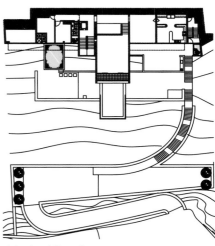

Living level floor plan

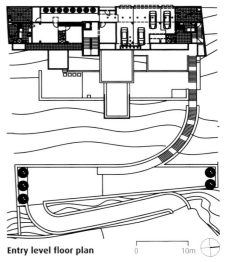

Entry level floor plan

0   10m

House K

Stocksund, Stockholm, Sweden

Tham & Videgård Hansson Arkitekter

Photography: Åke E:son Lindman

This two-story house in Stocksund appears as a narrow block with perforations inserted for light. Covering the full width of the property, it separates the east-facing front yard from the garden in the southwest. Through its position on the site, the house is experienced almost exclusively from the front angle, appearing deceptively as just a line or a wall.

The shallow block allows light to be introduced from several directions. The two levels also guide views and light diagonally through the interior. The plan is simple: the entry and stairs fit into one box on the ground level, and a central passage on the upper floor provides access to the bedrooms.

The interior is one continuous space, on two levels. As a result, movement through the house is characterized by visual shortcuts, spaces, and overlapping activities.

The main structure is in situ cast concrete, which is exposed in the cantilevered entrance canopy. Costs were reduced to not more than a standard-type house by using a system that combined the thermal insulation with the concrete formwork. The interior is finished with white plaster, and all floors and wooden details are white ash. The façades are black-stained plywood panels, mounted in layers on a pine framework.

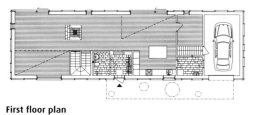

First floor plan

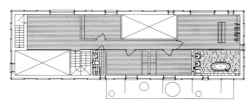

Second floor plan

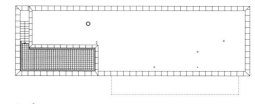

Roof terrace

House M

Amsterdam, The Netherlands

Marc Koehler Architects

Photography: Marcel van der Burg

This house in Almere, a satellite suburb of Amsterdam, is a contemporary response to a changing cultural environment in The Netherlands that is characterized by a growing demand for monumentality, solidity, and enclosure in the architecture of private houses.

The house is positioned like a wall between the front and back gardens, separating an introverted street façade from an extroverted garden façade (at the rear of the house). The kitchen, dining room, living room, and office are on the open-plan ground floor that opens up toward the sunny back garden. Three bedrooms, storage space, and a bathroom are on the second floor.

From the street, the house appears closed and monolithic. Two volumes reach out from this mass, providing the entrance and the garage space, and creating an interesting visual dialogue with the neighboring houses built in neo-classical style.

Passive solar energy design aspects reduce the requirement for active heating and cooling systems. An additional "playroom" volume at the back of the garden functions as a guest room and atelier, reinforcing the integration between the house and the garden landscape.

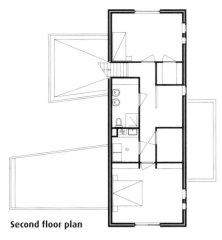

Second floor plan

First floor plan

House of Light

Seattle, Washington, USA

Olson Kundig Architects

Photography: Benjamin Benschneider and Paul Warchol

Nature, light, and art are integral elements contributing to the design of this house. Oriented east–west to optimize sun exposure, the house responds to its natural surroundings; the design becomes part of the landscape, facilitating movement inside and out.

The house's design was conceived as an extension of the garden, with both interior and exterior spaces intended to be quiet backdrops for the clients' art collection, which includes a 130-foot-long steel serpentine sculpture by Richard Serra. As a counterpoint to the solid outdoor structure, a spine-like band of light runs the length of the home's roof, culminating in a monumental installation by artist James Turrell.

Interior spaces are organized along a central two-story gallery, above which floats a fabric scrim that diffuses the light from clerestory windows and skylights. Full-height glass walls along the north and south façades allow light into the interior; the fabric-obscured clerestory, skylight, and glass walls create a balance of light within the center of the house, enhancing the experience of the art. Geothermal systems are used for heating and cooling. The buffalo grass-planted roof and trellises with hanging vines further integrate the home into the lush garden setting and provide sun shading in summer.

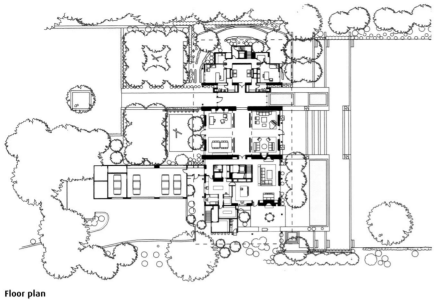

Floor plan

House on Hoopers Island

Church Creek, Maryland, USA

David Jameson Architect

Photography: Paul Warchol Photography

This 2,200-square-foot residence is located on a Chesapeake Bay barrier island near the Blackwater National Wildlife Refuge. The idea of an elemental architecture is explored in the relationship between the simple form of the building and the agrarian structures that dot the surrounding area.

The local vernacular of barns and fishing shacks provided inspiration for the new house, which was elevated using plinths made of black ground-face concrete masonry. The plinth foundations result in an opportunity to create above-ground structures such as the outdoor shower, the swimming pool, and the fire pit.

The house is composed of several separate cabins that can be locked down or conditioned and inhabited as needed. The master cabin and lodge are articulated as metal and wood tubes that cantilever off the plinths, minimizing their footprints. The guest cabin is located between the lodge and master cabin and has a roof that protrudes above the main roof to act as an abstracted light fixture, greeting visitors as they approach. A screened porch links the three volumes, while providing a breezy place to relax. A wood sun deck connects the pool plinth to the lodge. A fourth structure is an art studio.

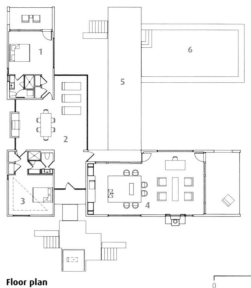

1 Master cabin
2 Screened porch
3 Guest cabin
4 Lodge
5 Sun deck
6 Pool
7 Art studio
8 Fire pit

Floor plan

0   15ft

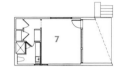

House Rieteiland

IJburg, Amsterdam, The Netherlands

Kirsten Gabriëls, James Webb

Photography: Marcel Van der Burg

A site with a south-facing view to a canal on the Grote Rietland of IJburg provided a unique opportunity for a family to live in a free-standing villa within 20 minutes of central Amsterdam.

The family of four required a house that provided opportunities for living together but also independently. The children are accommodated on the lower level, the parents on the upper, and the ground floor acts as the communal family and social area.

Similar to a typical Amsterdam canal house, the ground floor is raised, increasing privacy from the street. The raised ground floor allows clear views to the canal at the rear and accommodates the basement below. This visual connection to the canal is maintained at all times, through the open stairs to the upper level and the absence of any doors dividing the ground-floor area.

The lower level, complete with kitchenette and bathroom, is accessed from the street via external stairs and becomes an independent zone from the main house. The dividing wall between the bedrooms is non-load-bearing so that when the children leave the family home, the basement could be used and rented as a separate studio apartment.

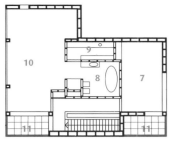

Second floor plan

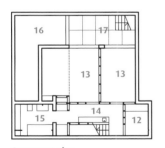

First floor plan

0   5m

Basement plan

1	Entry	10	Master bedroom
2	Living room	11	Balcony
3	Library	12	Utility
4	Dining	13	Children's room
5	Kitchen	14	Kitchenette
6	Terrace	15	Children's bathroom
7	Study	16	Storage
8	Bathroom	17	Below-ground terrace
9	Walk-in closet		

House SH

Minato-ku, Tokyo, Japan

Hiroshi Nakamura & NAP Architects

Photography: Daici Ano and NAP

This intriguing house is in a densely built residential area of Tokyo, and presented many challenges to the architect in relation to privacy and sunlight. The only open side of the site faces the north, where there is no direct sunlight. The south side faces the balcony and living room of an apartment next door, presenting privacy problems. Rather than inserting a large window that would have to remain covered for privacy reasons, the solution was to bring light into the building via a substantial skylight with a void extending from the top floor down to the basement.

To achieve this, the volume was raised up as high as possible after securing space for a car park; the wall was then pushed out as far as possible and a curved hollow was created in the wall.

The result is a mysterious shape, like a kangaroo's pouch, cloud-like from the inside. When light from the skylight above strikes this wall, a loss of distance perception seems to occur, bringing infinite depth into this small house. Sitting and lying in the recess created by the "pouch" on the inside, the occupants form an intimate connection with the hollow, a deliberate ploy of the architect, whose aim is to create intimacy between architecture and people.

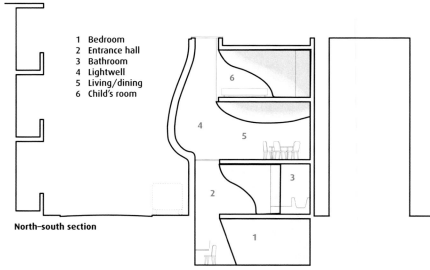

1 Bedroom
2 Entrance hall
3 Bathroom
4 Lightwell
5 Living/dining
6 Child's room

North–south section

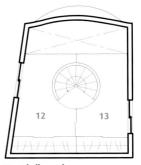

Fourth floor plan

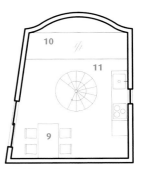

Third floor plan

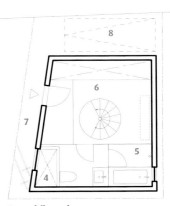

Second floor plan

First floor plan

1	Bedroom	8 Parking
2	Closet	9 Dining
3	Reading room	10 Living
4	Lightwell	11 Kitchen
5	Bathroom	12 Child's room 1
6	Entrance hall	13 Child's room 2
7	Bicycle parking	

Hudson-Panos House

Healdsburg, California, USA

Swatt | Miers Architects

Photography: Russell Abraham

This restful getaway is a place for a family to gather in a relaxing environment in the heart of California's wine country. The 2,900-square-foot house is set on a long, slender knoll on the 9-acre hillside property, bordered by Douglas fir, madrone, and mature oak trees on the east, south, and west sides, and with unobstructed views of the Dry Creek Valley to the north.

The plan consists of two parallel wings, slightly offset to create a linear courtyard. A detached carport anchors the east side of the house, while a 50-foot swimming pool terminates the linear composition to the west. The east wing contains the children's and guest bedrooms while the west wing contains public spaces on the lower level and the master bedroom suite on the upper level. A large, two-story volume with clerestory glazing creates an exciting vertical counterpoint to the mostly horizontal design, and bathes the interior with natural light.

The exterior palette includes gray integral-colored stucco, silver-painted aluminum-clad windows, and clear-finished 1x4 Western red cedar boards. Cedar is further applied to the soffits, ceilings, overhangs, and trellises. When combined with the exposed glue-laminated beams, these natural wood elements help to extend the views outward and blur the boundary between interior and exterior spaces.

North elevation

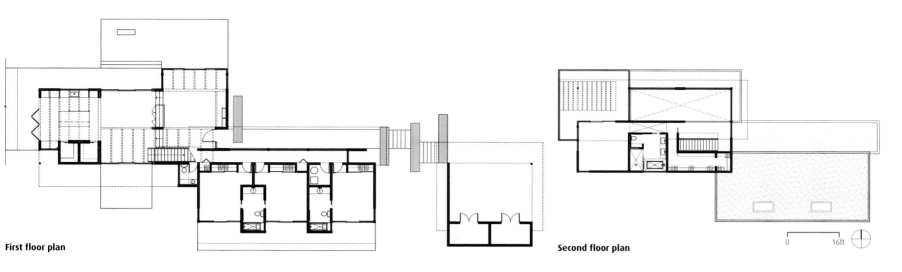

First floor plan

Second floor plan

0   16ft

IJburg House

Amsterdam, The Netherlands

Marc Koehler Architects;
Made-up interior works

Photography: Marcel van der Burg

This 1,500-square-foot house is located in IJburg, a recently developed suburb of Amsterdam. The house is designed as a vertical garden, to encourage flora and fauna to grow in a densely urbanized area.

Three bedrooms, a small bathroom, and a multipurpose area are situated on the first floor while the second floor, which is flooded with daylight, remains completely open for living, cooking, and eating. Storage and service spaces are invisibly integrated into thick walls, keeping the living spaces as open, transparent, and flexible as possible.

The façade contains traditional brick detailing inspired by techniques from the famous Amsterdam school style of the 1920s. The ornamental masonry also functions as an underlayer to support climbing plants that will over time overgrow the house and create a "natural curtain" around the living spaces and terraces, providing shading and privacy, and the opportunity to grow fruit.

The "living" green façade will change over time while giving space to birds and insects, creating a new urban ecosystem. Large windows capture sunlight to heat the interior in winter, and use the natural curtain to create shading in summer. The house also features a heating earth-pump and a ventilation system using a heat recovery unit, combined with natural ventilation in each space.

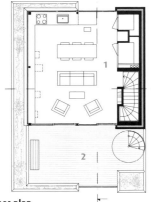

Second floor plan

1 Living
2 Terrace

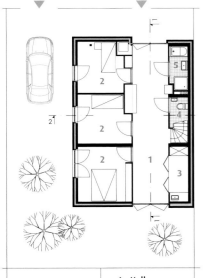

First floor plan

1 Hall
2 Bedroom
3 Storage room
4 WC
5 Bathroom

217

Jigsaw

Bethesda, Maryland, USA

David Jameson Architect

Photography: Nic Lehoux Photography

This project involved the "recycling" of a single-story suburban house on a busy corner site. The new house is a continuous spatial flow around an open-air courtyard carved from the home's remains. A matrix of spaces is linked by movement through them as different levels merge and spaces relate to each other as they rise and fall in a series of interlocked puzzle-like volumes. Particularity rather than repetition is employed, giving a unique three-dimensional framework to each space where plan and section respond to program simultaneously.

Fundamental to the conception of the house is the notion of reflectivity, rendering unclear the boundaries between inside and outside. Light and space are modulated by meshing ribbons of wall and glass that form a tessellation of solid and void.

The conditioning of these internal and external walls is identical. Planes of stucco exterior walls transform into plaster interior walls while passing through glass. Clerestory glazing and window constructs are carefully sited to afford privacy to the occupants while framing and extending views through the site.

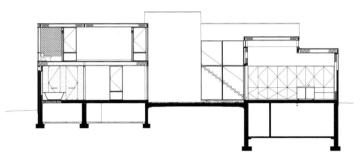

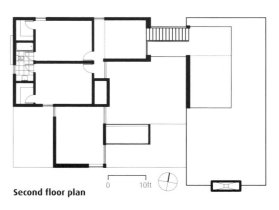

Second floor plan

0   10ft

First floor plan

Joanópolis House

Joanópolis, Brazil

Una Arquitetos

Photography: Bebete Viégas

This region of Brazil is at the foot of Mantiqueira Mountain, on the border of the states of São Paulo and Minas Gerais. The house is located along the banks of Piracaia Lake, near the village of Lopo.

The architects wanted to integrate the house with the surrounding topography and to protect it from the surrounding houses. To embed the house into the site, stone framing walls were built from locally collected rocks, using local techniques. Three interrelated courtyards were formed outside the inner rooms of the house.

The only part of the house visible from the street is the white tower (which contains the kitchen, chimneys, water tank, and heaters), which appears above the horizontal roof garden. An intermediate level between the street and the house is used for car parking. This level provides access to the roof garden and, via a tunnel, to the entrance gateway that leads to the courtyard outside the living room.

The house is well suited to many occupants engaged in different activities—the architects call it a "party house." During the day, the spaces open up completely to form a vast porch; by night they can be closed while maintaining transparency.

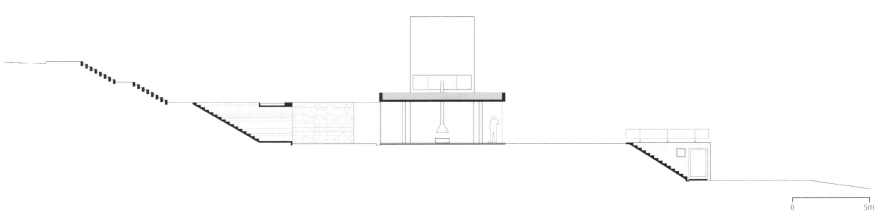

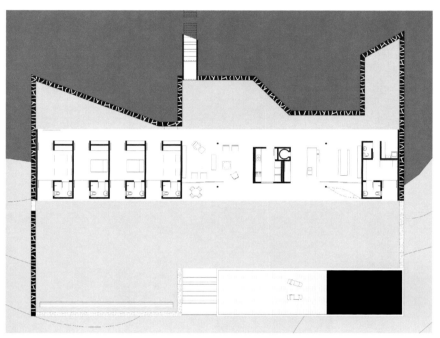

Second floor plan

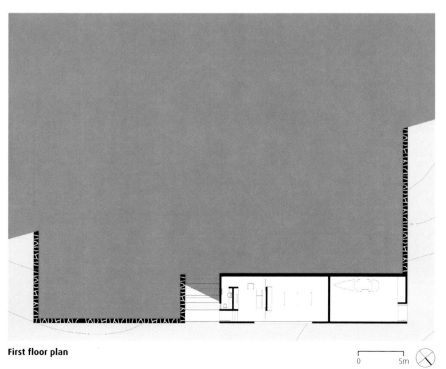

First floor plan

0   5m

225

Kumar Residence

New Delhi, India

Morphogenesis

Photography: Jatinder Marwaha

This house is located in an affluent neighborhood in the increasingly dense city of New Delhi. Though starkly modern, the design takes cues from Indian sanctuaries: the *haveli* or mansion organized around private courts, the step-well with an enfilade of semi-enclosed shaded spaces, and the temple sanctum, serene despite the chaos outside.

The fortress-like entrance wall is punctuated by a large opening that allows a glimpse of the entry courtyard. This forecourt, shaded by a tree in a bed of white pebbles, establishes the minimalist mood of the residence. The interior is animated through skylit courts where filtered sunlight continuously changes the feel of the space through the day and the seasons. Large picture windows and glass walls allow space to flow uninterrupted from the inside to the outside without the mediation of frames. Concealed cove lighting behind the floating ceiling in the living room washes the walls in a gentle glow.

Rich materials contrast with the spare austerity of the interiors. Polished concrete, glass, polished ebony, and stainless steel surfaces play off each other, bringing texture and lightness to the spaces and providing a tactile and sensual counterpoint to the white architectural surfaces. Woods as varied as walnut and wenge are juxtaposed to pick up their individual grain and textural nuances.

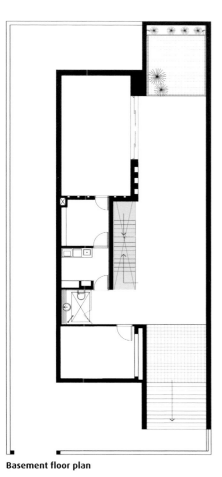

Basement floor plan

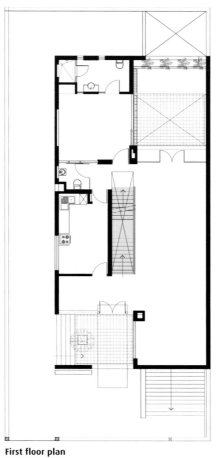

First floor plan

Second floor plan

227

L House

Zollikon, Switzerland

Philippe Stuebi Architekten

Photography: Dominique Marc Wehrli

This house, in an affluent suburb of Zurich, replaces a previous house on the site. The brief for the new house included fairly standard requirements such as a fitness room, open-plan kitchen, elevator, and underground garage. The unusual aspect of the brief was accommodation for the clients' collection of many thousands of rare books.

The triangular site, and various zoning and building restrictions, dictated the shape of the house. The architect's concept was one of continuous movement throughout the house, stretching and extending the spaces according to classical enfilade principles.

Each room is unique in size and form: the entry is conical, the entrance hall is a double-story cube, the loggia is triangular, and the library has a curved, glazed wall. Several balconies extend the floor area and allow stunning views of the surrounding landscape, which includes Lake Zurich and The Alps.

The three-sided glazing of the library on the ground floor is mirrored-glass, which protects the books from damaging UV rays. Depending on the time of day and the lighting conditions, either the stored books or the reflected garden are visible. The upper floors are completed in bright lime rendering and the windows in natural anodized aluminum.

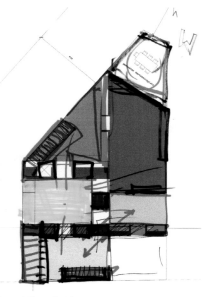

Ground floor sketch

Laidley Residence

San Francisco, California, USA

Zack/de Vito Architecture

Photography: Bruce Damonte

This new, ground-up single-family residence peers over a steep downhill slope where views of the city are omnipresent. Light floods through the translucent stair lighting the core of the three levels. The open plan is composed rationally as two side-by-side sliding volumes whose larger volume pushes further out toward the view. Using a consistent palette of materials and detailing techniques, the project exemplifies craft.

The house uses current techniques of sustainable design and construction with high fly ash concrete, engineered lumber, FSC-certified woods, and palm wood flooring, among others. The house is fully powered by PV panels and solar hot water panels. Using panelized construction, 80 percent of the framing was built off-site and delivered to the site and craned into place.

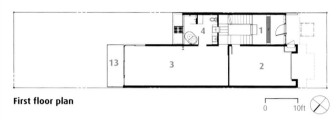

Second floor plan

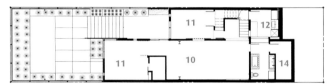

First floor plan

0   10ft

Basement floor plan

1	Entry	8	Living
2	Garage	9	Sitting
3	Master suite	10	Family
4	Bathroom	11	Bedroom
5	Guest room	12	Laundry
6	Kitchen	13	Deck
7	Dining	14	Mechanical

Lake Calhoun Residence

Minneapolis, Minnesota, USA

Charles R. Stinson Architects

Photography: Paul Crosby Architectural Photography

The clients desired a multi-generational home like an Armani suit; simple and functional, yet brought to the level of art through the use of luxurious materials and harmonic proportions. Through landscaping and careful siting this house achieves privacy without sacrificing warmth or the dramatic views toward the lake.

Beyond the granite site walls, the monolithic limestone panel shell of the home gracefully folds open to reveal teak wood siding and glimpses of the warm interior material palette. The U-shaped plan forms a private auto court with 40 geothermal wells below the granite pavers for heating and cooling the house. A three-story glass stair tower anchors the folding limestone forms and spirals up to a green rooftop terrace complete with a fireplace and views of downtown Minneapolis. The green roof filters and collects water for irrigating the lawn and the rest of the roof is prepared for future photovoltaic panels.

The program includes a state-of-the-art fitness room, a spacious wine cellar, four bedroom suites each with private baths, and a master suite nested into the most secluded wing of the home. The bedrooms overlook the lake, the downtown skyline, and an edgeless swimming pool adorned in very small reflective blue tiles.

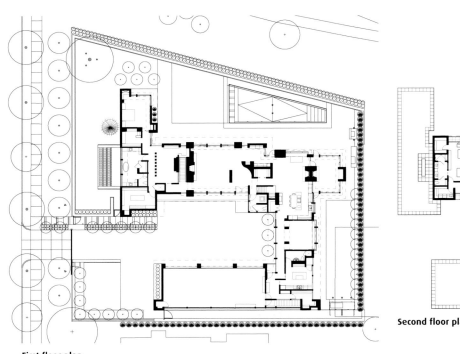

First floor plan

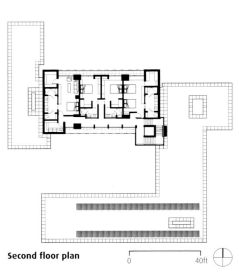

Second floor plan

0   40ft

Lake House

Strathallan Woods, Ontario, Canada

Kohn Shnier Architects

Photography: Ben Rahn/A Frame

Comfortable enough for two, but able to accommodate 20, this new home is on an elevated site with views toward a large lake. At just over 4,000 square feet, the floor plan is large but efficient.

The house can be described as a four-level, single-story volume. The levels eliminate long lengths of stairs and create many interesting spatial opportunities and views through the house. The first-level bedrooms face a garden court and are enveloped in three types of glass that reflect and diffuse the cedar hedge defining the garden. The adjoining circulation hallway provides access between these bedrooms and a string of bathrooms. The last layer comprises the public spaces—living, dining, and

TV/games room. This last room is slightly depressed into the ground, creating an intimate environment for lounging; the master bedroom is above, nestled in the treetops with a beautiful view of the lake.

The house structure combines steel framing and wood stress panels to maximize spans yet maintain an economic skeleton. A large roof overhang creates a perimeter terrace that shades the exposed glass surface and provides shelter from the weather. Exterior materials include cement board siding with clear and reflective curtain wall; interior finishes are concrete, oiled oak, and white marble.

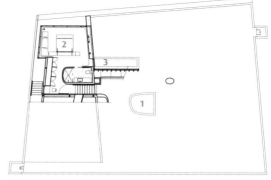

1 Light court
2 Master bedroom
3 Skylight over outdoor dining

Second floor plan

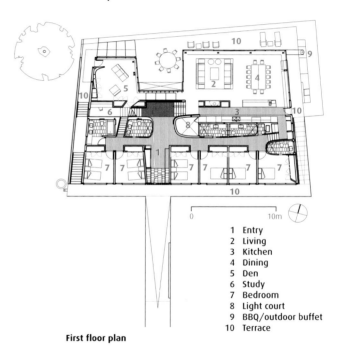

0   10m

1 Entry
2 Living
3 Kitchen
4 Dining
5 Den
6 Study
7 Bedroom
8 Light court
9 BBQ/outdoor buffet
10 Terrace

First floor plan

Lake Walen House

Lake Walen, Switzerland

K_M Architektur

Photography: courtesy K_M Architektur

This modernist house in the Swiss Alps has an unrivalled position, with unobstructed views of Lake Walen and the Churfirsten mountain range.

The site, on the slope of a green meadow, offered perfect conditions to build a design that appears to float, through its clear form and the use of natural materials—including concrete, glass, and wood, as structural elements.

A loggia encircles the building on the water side, extending the open living space and creating a flowing transition between interior and exterior with a fantastic panoramic view. Floor-to-ceiling sliding glass doors intensify the effect on the view side while the back of the house has a more closed appearance. Rooftop photovoltaic panels and a stove in the living room produce most of the energy for the home.

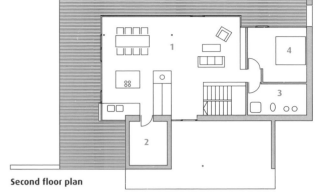

Second floor plan

1 Kitchen/living/dining
2 Pantry
3 Bathroom
4 Bedroom

First floor plan

1 Study
2 Bathroom
3 Storage
4 Bedroom

0   2m

Lobster Boat House

Seattle, Washington, USA

chadbourne + doss architects

Photography: Benjamin Benschneider

Located on a dense urban shoreline site, this economical, purposeful, and durable residence strives to celebrate its location while providing privacy to its occupants. Built on an existing floor and foundation infrastructure, the constraints of site and footprint result in an efficient vertical house that reaches the maximum allowable zoning envelope to provide a variety of indoor and outdoor spaces.

This major remodel project utilizes as much of the existing structure as possible, such as concrete foundations, wood framing, and existing utilities.

Features that make the new residence more energy efficient include hydronic heating in the floors, high R-value foam insulation, modular cabinetry, low-flush toilets, passive solar, and day-lighting strategies. Green materials include integral color cement board siding, recycled structural lumber, reclaimed wood flooring, low-VOC finishes, single membrane roofing, cement plaster floors and walls, and pre-wiring for future solar roof panels.

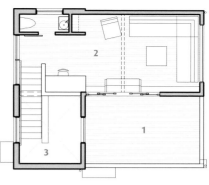

1 Roof deck
2 Lounge
3 Open to below

Third floor plan

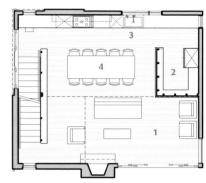

1 Living
2 Pantry
3 Kitchen
4 Dining

Second floor plan

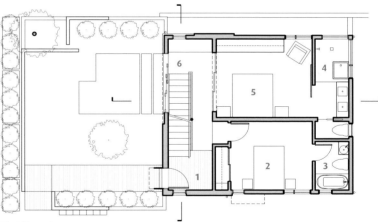

First floor plan

1 Entry
2 Bedroom
3 Bathroom
4 Master bathroom
5 Master bedroom
6 Hall

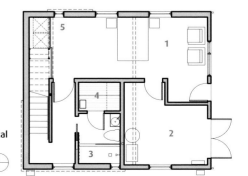

1 Guest bedroom
2 Storage/mechanical
3 Bathroom
4 Sauna
5 Laundry

Basement floor plan

Love House

Yokohama, Kanagawa, Japan

Takeshi Hosaka

Photography: Masao Nishikawa and
Nacasa & Partners

This house is in Isogo-ku, Yokahama, a 30-minute train trip from Tokyo. The very small site has a frontage of only 11 feet and is just 33 feet deep. The house takes up most of the site.

The clients' wish was to be able to enjoy nature from within the house. Thus, the architect planned as many spaces as possible to be open to the outdoors, with minimal distinctions between the inside and outside. The elements are exposed via the curved roof opening above the stair, creating spaces that are neither "inside" nor "outside." Sunlight entering through the opening animates the space during the day; at night, the space is lit by moonlight or by candlelight—there is no electrical lighting to detract from the ever-changing effects of nature. Birds and insects are invited into the house to coexist with the occupants, who decided to forego a television in favor of the rich experiences they gain from being at one with nature. A special area was designed for the clients' pet rabbit.

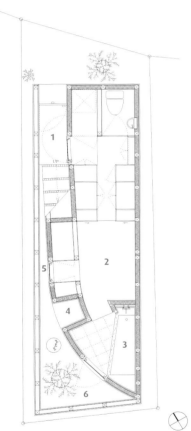

First floor plan   Second floor plan

1 Entry
2 Bedroom
3 Bathroom
4 Rabbit space
5 Rabbit way
6 Garden
7 Terrace
8 Living
9 Kitchen

L-Stack House

Fayetteville, Arkansas, USA

Marlon Blackwell Architect

Photography: Timothy Hursley

This house was designed in response to the anomalies of the trapezoid-shaped site, set within a dense inner-city neighborhood near a city park, and traversed diagonally by a seasonal creek. The L-shaped configuration subdivides the interior program and the site into private and public entities. A carefully positioned glass-enclosed stairway hinges together the two 18-foot-wide boxes that form the house structure.

Inside, the ground floor is organized as a linear open plan with connecting terraces along and adjacent to the creek. Throughout the house, windows and skylights are arranged to provide controlled views, illumination, a sense of privacy, and opportunities to observe the dynamic nature of the creek. On the second floor, all spaces open onto a hall that serves as a common family space for reading, office work, or watching television.

Primary interior materials include teak floors, wenge, walnut, and white oak millwork, and painted wood plank accent walls. The exterior cladding is a unique rain screen system articulated with rot-resistant Brazilian redwood. The cladding system provides for 50 percent transparency and perceptually provides the walls with remarkable translucency. End walls are either black metal-clad or glass storefronts.

First floor plan

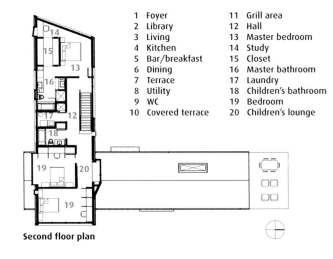

1 Foyer	11 Grill area
2 Library	12 Hall
3 Living	13 Master bedroom
4 Kitchen	14 Study
5 Bar/breakfast	15 Closet
6 Dining	16 Master bathroom
7 Terrace	17 Laundry
8 Utility	18 Children's bathroom
9 WC	19 Bedroom
10 Covered terrace	20 Children's lounge

Second floor plan

247

Lyndhurst Way

London, UK

Richard Dudzicki Associates Ltd

Photography: Robert Parrish/Valency Engine

This major renovation began as a project to create a new, contemporary basement extension to open up the back of this Grade II listed early Victorian house. It grew to encompass every room in the house and included creating new bathrooms, redesigning the bedrooms to include more storage, and interior design aspects.

The design involved pulling the new extension away from the existing building with the use of a glass skylight. The plateau double-glazed skylight brings in more light and acts as a junction between the old and the new. The basement roof is covered with sedum so the view from the original grand ground-floor living room, at the rear of the property, is of a green plane that continues into the vista of the garden, and not of a flat roof.

The contemporary extension opens out the entire basement floor, allowing the garden to flow back into the house and creating a very comfortable open-plan living/dining area. The use of paneled zinc cladding to cover the extension provides a counterpoint to the 19th-century brickwork. The startling interior with a striking modern white kitchen with magenta glass splashback contrasts with the traditional restored original features that still exist within the building.

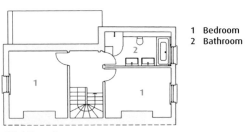

Third floor plan

1 Bedroom
2 Bathroom

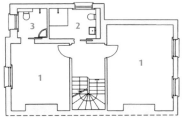

Second floor plan

1 Bedroom
2 Bathroom
3 Wetroom

First floor plan

1 Hallway
2 TV room
3 Living
4 Sedum roof

Basement floor plan

1	Study	7	WC
2	Storage	8	Kitchen/lounge
3	Hallway	9	Sunken garden
4	Laundry	10	Large seating steps
5	Bathroom	11	Garden
6	Utility		

0   4m

Maison de la Lumière

Bologna, Italy

Damilano Studio Architects

Photography: Andrea Martiradonna

The design of this house is focused on the impact of light and the resulting effects on lines, colors, and shapes. Two fundamental requirements of the clients were to avoid the stereotypical housing of the area and to build a technologically advanced house.

The rooms are arranged in a continuous sequence: the bathroom opens into the bedroom, the kitchen into the living room, and the living room rises toward the loft, creating spatial and visual continuity. The double-height living room, with its glazed roof and generous windows, has the feel of a glass cube.

The lightness of the construction is counteracted by the materiality of the stone wall at the entrance, complemented by an ipe wood footbridge. Slatted wood elements and sliding panels create mobile wings that shield the more private rooms.

A domotic system, which can operate remotely, manages household functions, ensuring security, climate control, and energy saving. The furniture reflects the characteristics of the house and features bright and delicate colors. Floors reflect light entering from the large windows and the walls are bright white. A surprising feature is the main bathroom, which is equipped with a floor-level Jacuzzi, illuminated from below by immersed spotlights.

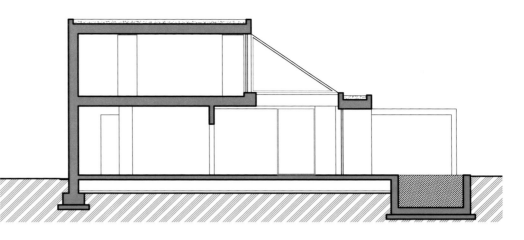

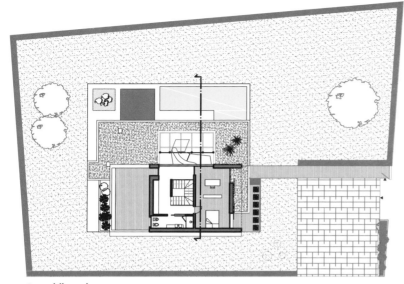

Second floor plan

First floor plan

Maytree House

Wicklow, Ireland

ODOS Architects

Photography: Ros Kavanagh and
ODOS Architects

This simple, bold sculptural form sits at the foot of a steep escarpment in the Wicklow hills. It replaces a derelict 1940s single-story cottage (with associated outhouses) that previously existed on the site.

Entry at first-floor level is via a long stepped processional route to the front of the building. The façade to this stepped approach has been purposely left blank to focus on the point of entry while also weighting the propped cantilever appropriately. At entry level a hallway precedes the open-plan living, kitchen, and dining areas, which are contained within the propped cantilevered volume that hovers above the landscape below.

A forest of red columns has been inserted below the cantilever, which conceptually grow out of the hillside. These columns "guard" a pedestrian route, which leads under the cantilever to the rear garden and living room deck at first-floor level. Along this route one truly experiences the sheerness of the escarpment above.

The roofscape is peppered with skylights in an attempt to engage the occupants with the steep escarpment to the rear of the house. They also afford unexpected vertical views of sky and foliage from the most private spaces within the house.

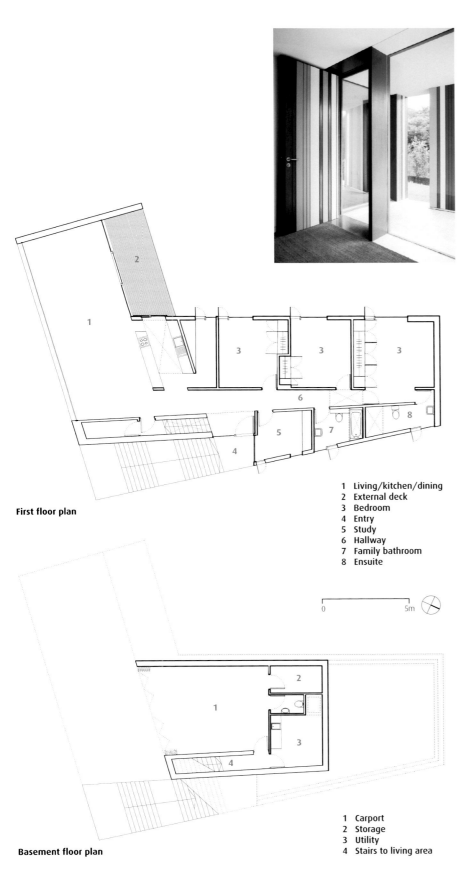

First floor plan

1 Living/kitchen/dining
2 External deck
3 Bedroom
4 Entry
5 Study
6 Hallway
7 Family bathroom
8 Ensuite

0 ——————— 5m

Basement floor plan

1 Carport
2 Storage
3 Utility
4 Stairs to living area

Mews House 03

Notting Hill Gate, London, UK

Andy Martin Associates

Photography: Nick Rochowski

This single-family residence is set in fashionable Notting Hill Gate. The owners wanted an existing two-level modest mews house to be redeveloped into a four-level family home. They desired the effect of a private cocoon that was also open to the elements.

The architects have creatively captured the available natural light by the use of glazing, wooden screens, and natural vegetation screens, conveying a unique atmosphere to all spaces, day and night.

The circulation through the levels is a critical element of the project. The circulation space is as long as reasonably possible. With sharp changes of direction, the circulation traverses the dimensions of the available volume, providing a powerful sequence of views in the process. The surface materials provide an experience of movement through the building, mapping out the route with a slippery black glazed monolith rising through the four levels.

One of the abutting walls, clad with Douglas fir, gives the impression that the building is somehow fixed back to a neatly constructed barn.

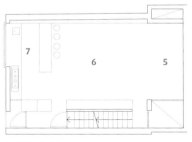

Third floor plan

Second floor plan

First floor plan

Basement floor plan

1	Lightwell
2	Cinema lounge
3	Bathroom
4	Mechanical
5	Conservatory
6	Living
7	Kitchen
8	Bedroom
9	Balcony

Moir Residence

Carmel, California, USA

Moore Ruble Yudell Architects & Planners

Photography: David O. Marlow

The design concept and spatial organization of this 5,000-square-foot residence are inspired by its immediate adjacency to an old-growth California oak woodland environment. The individual locations of the 150-year-old trees offered key design clues in the placement of the programmatic elements of the home within its natural environment. The design concept weaves building mass within the woodland environment into one composition, framing views of the landscape, both near and far. Ridges, valleys, and rock outcrops become key focal elements in the experience of the home both inside and out. The roof planes and profiles of the residence mimic the surrounding regional topography, while the varied shapes of the multi-colored blue slate roof resonate with the changing colors of the natural environment. Light monitors rise above the rooflines and treetops to receive the gentle northern daylight.

A crescent-shaped courtyard weaves in and around the trees at the entry to the home. The H-shaped plan frames two central courtyards, which form part of a landscape path that moves from hilltop to stream. Existing trees in the woodland are preserved and integrated into a dynamic relationship between the natural and built environments.

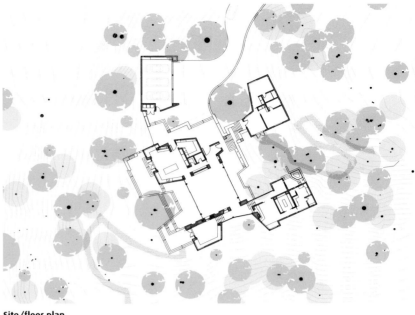

Site/floor plan

Moko House

Torquay, Victoria, Australia

Peter Winkler Architects

Photography: Ferne Millen Photography and Cormac Hanrahan

This house was created to embody the clients' love of the beach. They wanted a house that was warm and sheltered in winter, while open and light-filled in summer.

The rural site slopes south to north toward a creek located off the property, with a treed gully to the east. The house both nestles into the existing topography and floats above it, wrapping around the site's contours and opening to natural ground level at various access points.

The building is stretched out along an east–west axis to allow maximum north light in. A sense of additional space is created by adjoining indoor or outdoor spaces. Living, gallery, and master bedroom spaces all open to decking through glazing. "Shoji" screens allow the central bedrooms to open to the gallery space, running alongside a Japanese garden. Slot windows offer further connections to the landscape.

Efficient spatial planning, the ability to isolate different zones, and large eaves were utilized to control the heating and cooling loads throughout the building. The east glazing of the living zone is also protected from hot summer sunlight by the hill on the site, while winter sunlight filters through the trees.

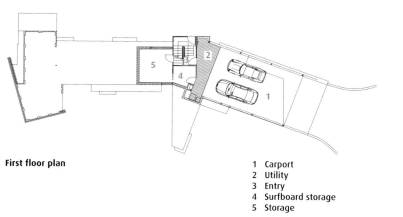

First floor plan

1 Carport
2 Utility
3 Entry
4 Surfboard storage
5 Storage

Second floor plan

1 Entry
2 Kitchen
3 Living
4 Dining
5 Void
6 Bedroom
7 Laundry

8 Bathroom
9 WC
10 Gallery
11 Master bedroom
12 Ensuite
13 Study
14 Deck

Montecito Residence

Montecito, California, USA

Olson Kundig Architects

Photography: Jim Bartsch; Nikolas Koenig; Tim Bies/Olson Kundig Architects

This single-family home is set in fire-prone Toro Canyon. The owners wanted a house that minimized its use of scarce natural resources and recognized the challenging environmental conditions of the area. The design solution was to create a house that could harvest and control the climatic conditions that make the site so dangerous—the sun and the wind.

The raised roof functions as an umbrella to shield the house from the sun, while the long central hallway allows naturally cool offshore breezes to move through the space. A 15-foot-tall Dutch door permits breezes to escape while maintaining a degree of privacy. The hallway also creates an axis dividing the private from the public. To the east lies the public entrance, garage, and road; to the west is a garden, pool, and guest rooms. The house is made of simple, fire-resistant materials. Steel is allowed to oxidize and concrete is toned to allow the house to blend into the landscape.

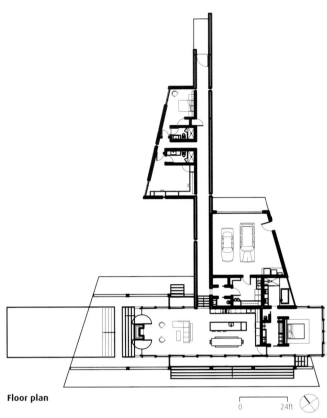

Floor plan

0   24ft

Muted House

Jakarta, Indonesia

Aboday Architect

Photography: Happy Lim Photography

This house, close to the Jakarta central business district, and adjoining a busy road, is not the ideal location for a family with three growing children. Thus, the main design challenge was to provide ample play and activity space for the children.

The clients were happy for the house to have an understated appearance. Its muted angular prismatic façade is painted in a textured warm gray; this austere face is peppered with random tiny squares of glass on one side. The muted appearance is echoed by the stark, all-white internal walls.

What the house lacks in terms of exterior play areas is well compensated for inside. To create a space that can be used as an indoor playground, the architects split the house into two main blocks. The wide gap between the blocks results in lofty voids above a wide connecting "bridge." The bridge, overlooking the dining room below, is an airy and bright space (thanks to the skylight above) that connects the kitchen to the children's room, which itself is like a floating playground. Using the principle of borrowed space, all bedrooms open onto the central lofty voids. A 6-foot-wide plunge pool slots into a residual space at the corner of the family room.

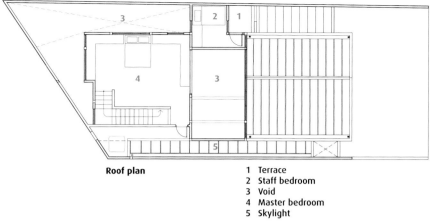

Roof plan

1 Terrace
2 Staff bedroom
3 Void
4 Master bedroom
5 Skylight

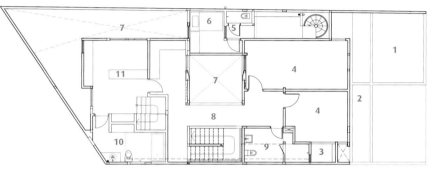

Second floor plan

1 Canopy
2 Skylight
3 Terrace
4 Child's bedroom
5 Staff bathroom
6 Staff bedroom
7 Void
8 Bridge
9 Bathroom
10 Master bathroom
11 Closet

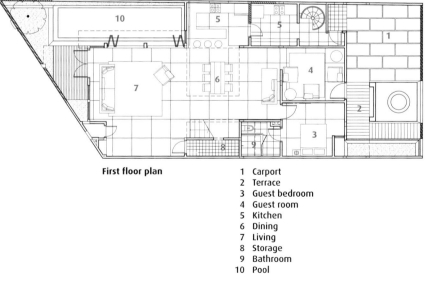

First floor plan

1 Carport
2 Terrace
3 Guest bedroom
4 Guest room
5 Kitchen
6 Dining
7 Living
8 Storage
9 Bathroom
10 Pool

N85 Residence

New Delhi, India

Morphogenesis

Photography: Amit Mehra,
André J Fanthome, and Edmund Sumner

This house sets out to create its own terrain, a veritable oasis, within its inscribed territory. The forecourt is landscaped with gracious steps and pools. Crisp clear planes are articulated with materials including stone, wood, and concrete, which are simply striated or set in interlocking patterns. Transparency is achieved not only by glass, but through water, reflection, and modulated lighting.

The residence multitasks as a house for three generations of a family and their many visitors, a busy workspace, and on occasion a cultural hub. Overlapping spatial categories are split into three levels: the private domain of the nuclear family (bedrooms and breakfast room), the shared intergenerational spaces such as the family room, kitchen, and dining areas, and the fluid public domain of the lobby and living spaces.

Moving through the house, it is clear that the central space is the fulcrum of the project. Circular skylights dot the ceiling and an interior garden beneath is a green sanctuary within the house. A lap pool fed by harvested rainwater runs the length of the terrace on the second floor.

Passive energy strategies include high thermal mass in the west, earth damping for the basement studios, landscape buffers on the south, and high-performance surfaces on the east.

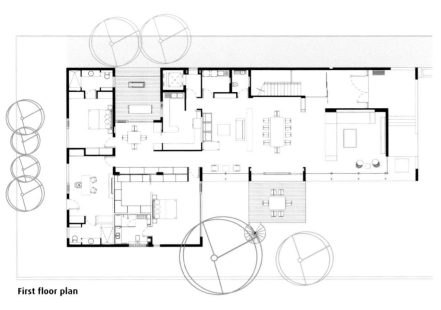

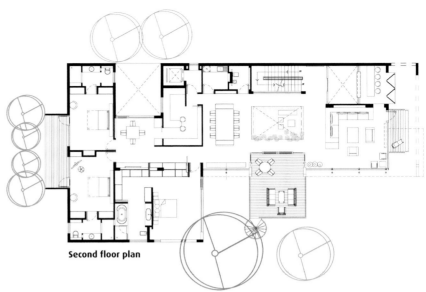

First floor plan

Second floor plan

271

Necklace House

Yamagata, Japan

Hiroshi Nakamura & NAP Architects

Photography: Daici Ano and NAP

The site of this 4,500-square-foot home for a family of six is located deep in the countryside. To counter heavy snowfall in winter, which can be up to 6 feet deep, the rooms "float" above the ground by means of the structural wall. The detached rooms are spread along the wall so that they can enjoy views of the garden and the nature outside. By arranging the rooms so that they are connected behind the wall, although each room appears to be detached, the family can move around the house without having to go outside. This arrangement of rooms as autonomous units contrasts with the conventional Japanese "madori" method where a large space is divided into small, oppressive rooms.

Although the rooms have individual characteristics—such as the timber bedroom with large trusses, the Japanese-style room, and the bathroom with 1,600 "windows," they are united like a necklace strung with different beads, hence the name of the house.

One of the most unique features of the house is the guest bathroom, which is clad in steel plate coated with fiberglass-reinforced plastic (FRP). Sunlight pours into the bathroom through holes punched in the steel plate, creating a dazzling array of sunspots that animate the space.

Second floor plan

1 Entry
2 Japanese-style room
3 Walk-in closet
4 Master bedroom
5 Utility
6 Bathroom
7 Living and dining
8 Kitchen
9 Bar
10 Pantry
11 Children's bedroom

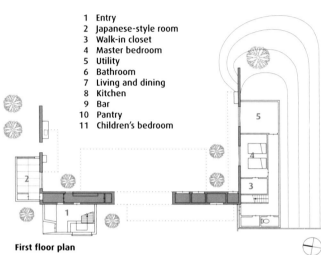

First floor plan

New Moon Residence

United Arab Emirates

Ehrlich Architects

Photography: Erhard Pfeiffer
and Irfan Naqi

Islamic culture is embodied and reinterpreted through modern technology and design in this 35,000-square-foot residence. Ample desalinated water allowed the desert site to be transformed into an oasis with pools and landscaping.

A massive curved aluminum roof shelters and unites the compound's series of two-story buildings. In section, the canopy forms a crescent moon, the symbol of new life that tops the minarets of Islam. The canopy is supported by stone-clad columns that function as mechanical exhaust vents. The whole structure suggests a giant Bedouin tent, with the football-field-sized roof, cantilevered 30 feet on each side, casting a giant swathe of shade.

A reflecting pool, which flows indoors and provides cooling, surrounds the front façade. A *mashrabiya*, the traditional lattice sunscreen, filters direct sun. Gardens, fountains, shady courtyards, and terraces surround and penetrate the buildings, making it a desert paradise.

The three-part plan separates the reception area (*majlis*) for male guests at the west from the women's area behind the central grand hall and the family's sleeping quarters to the east. In a dance between ancient and modern, massive stone walls are counterpoint to large expanses of glass and taut elements of steel.

The executive architect for this project was Godwin Austen Johnson.

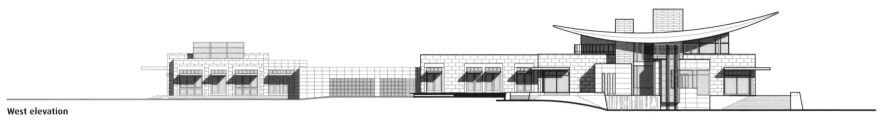

West elevation

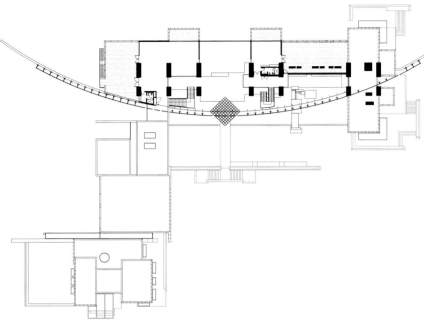

Second floor plan

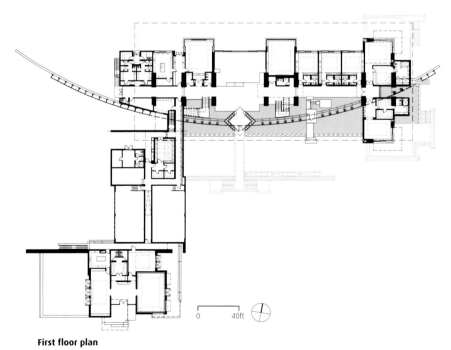

First floor plan

0   40ft

Nighthawk Retreat

Washington, USA

Eggleston Farkas Architects

Photography: Jim Van Gundy

The site for this family vacation retreat is on a remote south-facing ridge along the eastern foothills of the Cascade Mountains. Wind-driven snowy winters and hot arid summers with occasional brush fires characterize the severe climate.

The brief was for a secluded house with a close connection to the natural environment. Because no public utilities were available, solar electrical generation and energy conservation were critical to the success of the project.

The V-shaped house is cut into the ridge, allowing for an earth-sheltered passive solar design. The concrete roof and retaining walls allowed the house to be buried under 4 feet of earth—offering insulation in the winter and cave-like cooling in summer. Concrete overhangs provide snow control and solar shading. Rolling metal shutters serve the dual purposes of forming a second skin, which offers additional thermal control, as well as fire protection and security when the retreat is not in use.

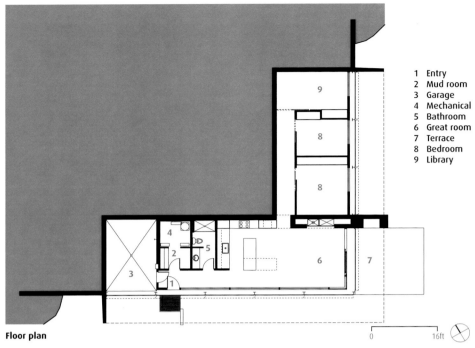

1 Entry
2 Mud room
3 Garage
4 Mechanical
5 Bathroom
6 Great room
7 Terrace
8 Bedroom
9 Library

Floor plan

0   16ft

Nourse Residence

Montecito, California, USA

The Warner Group Architects, Inc.

Photography: Lawrence Anderson

This 7,200-square-foot contemporary residence is located on a hilltop in Montecito, California. The sizable living room opens up to a covered veranda by way of floor-to-ceiling glass pocket doors. The veranda's expansive framed openings capture the site's panoramic ocean to mountain views and can be completely enclosed with exterior draperies for nighttime dining and entertaining. Blooming lotus plants and an oak-tree canopy surround the swimming pool beyond the veranda.

On the interior, tall, broad, white walls in the gallery accommodate the owners' vast art collection, which is naturally illuminated with strategically placed skylights. A floor-to-ceiling frameless glass wall just off the wood-paneled study highlights an infinity-edge reflecting pool. Strong, clean lines complement the owners' eclectic collection of furniture and artwork.

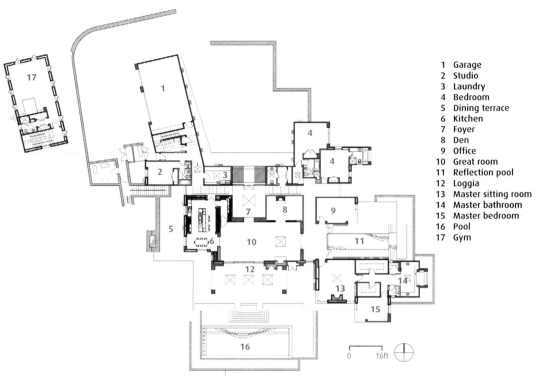

1 Garage
2 Studio
3 Laundry
4 Bedroom
5 Dining terrace
6 Kitchen
7 Foyer
8 Den
9 Office
10 Great room
11 Reflection pool
12 Loggia
13 Master sitting room
14 Master bathroom
15 Master bedroom
16 Pool
17 Gym

0   16ft

Floor plan

Noyack Creek Residence

Noyack, New York, USA

Bates Masi Architects

Photography: courtesy Bates Masi Architects

The client sought a place for relaxation and casual entertaining on a deep, narrow lot fronting the tidal estuary of Noyack Creek. The site's wetlands and zoning setbacks dictated much of the design.

Spaces tailored to the daily routine are coiled hierarchically around a double-height kitchen "core" permeated by light and air from clerestories above. Unexpected moments arise where this coil doubles back on itself; for example, the interior stair to the second floor and the exterior stair to the roof deck directly parallel one another. A catwalk bridges the double-height space above the kitchen, providing access to the master bedroom while serving as an eyrie from which to survey the spaces below.

The walls enclosing these spaces are made with panels of a natural resin composite commonly used in sports arenas. By pre-cutting and perforating this material with a water-jet it can be made tightly seamed and solid for privacy, while at other times loosely positioned and frequently pierced to allow the passage of light and air.

The west glass façade allows every room to overlook the creek and summer sunsets—even from the first floor, elevated on tall foundation walls to sit above of the rolling hills approaching the water's edge.

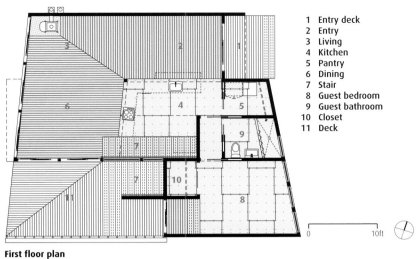

First floor plan

1 Entry deck
2 Entry
3 Living
4 Kitchen
5 Pantry
6 Dining
7 Stair
8 Guest bedroom
9 Guest bathroom
10 Closet
11 Deck

0   10ft

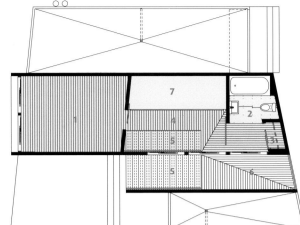
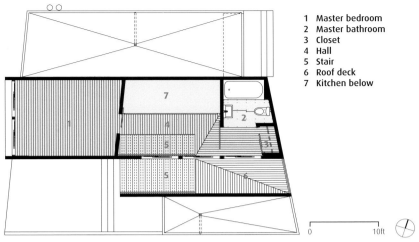

Second floor plan

1 Master bedroom
2 Master bathroom
3 Closet
4 Hall
5 Stair
6 Roof deck
7 Kitchen below

0   10ft

287

O House

Lake Lucerne, Switzerland

Philippe Stuebi Architekten

Photography: Dominique Marc Wehrli

This sculptural villa is defined by its expressive and ornamental façades. Facing Mount Pilatus, the white concrete elements are dotted with circular openings that allow glimpses into the two-level orangery with its exotic plants, as well as the lounge, the guest area, and the staircase, accessed through one of the openings at the ground floor.

The house's lake façade has superb mountain views of the Rigi and the Bürgenstock and features a protruding, glistening loggia made of round glass bricks. These highly decorative elements are a strong contrast to the rough renderings of the side façades. The basement nestles along the slope and opens into a large fitness area with a 25-meter pool—half indoors, half outdoors—which is inserted in a white terrazzo plate. This terrazzo plate extends gracefully from the pool bar, located inside the white-tinted, rough jetted concrete boathouse, into Lake Lucerne.

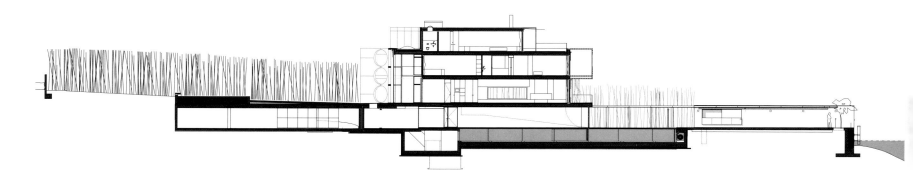

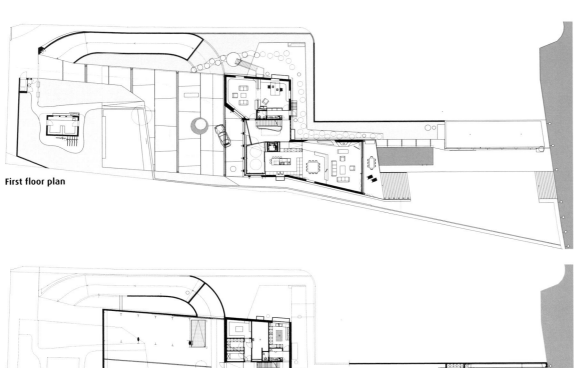

First floor plan

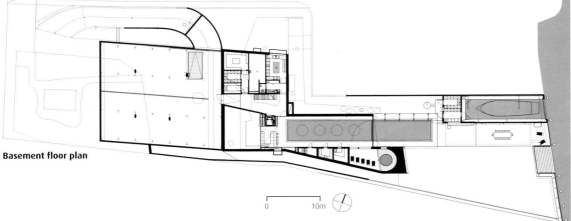

Basement floor plan

0   10m

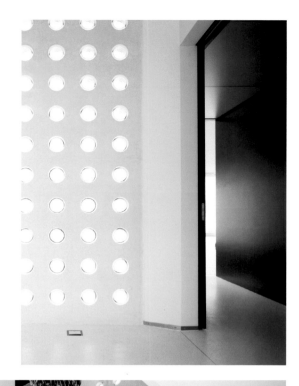

Oaklands House

Johannesburg, South Africa

AMA Architects

Photography: Dalton Dingelstad

This substantial home of more than 10,000 square feet is located in Oaklands, a leafy suburb of Johannesburg.

The brief was the result of an extensive consultation with an informed client who has traveled extensively. The client had developed an appreciation of the simplicity of the architecture of single-volume homes, and their uniquely liberating, spacious feel.

Because the brief was volumetric in nature, the architects designed the house from the inside out, providing an interaction of scales experienced from arrival through to repose. These are the staged processional experiences gained from entering the home through to its heart.

The house is a place to come home to, and a space in which to enjoy high levels of contemporary refinement, art, and technology—a house in pursuit of happiness. Special features include an interior balcony that overlooks the loft living space, much like the bridge of a great ship.

Interior spaces designed by AMA Architects and D12 Interiors represent a successful collaboration of architecture and interior architecture, projecting a richness of scale, purpose, and place.

Second floor plan

1 Home cinema
2 Master bedroom
3 Bathroom
4 Bedroom
5 Reading area

First floor plan

1	Entry	7	Playroom
2	Lounge	8	Guest room
3	Study	9	Bathroom
4	Dining	10	Staff accommodation
5	Kitchen	11	Garage
6	Patio	12	WC

Old Greenwich Residence

Southport, Connecticut, USA

Austin Patterson Disston Architects

Photography: Durston Saylor

The design of this new five-bedroom house centered on providing direct waterfront views. The site was tight, with the neighbor's house extremely close to the water's edge and in danger of obstructing views. The clients wanted as many rooms as possible to face the view in addition to an expansive waterside yard for full enjoyment of the water and to accommodate the many sports activities of their children.

The solution was a semicircular house, taking its planning and design cues from the work of Edwin Lutyens and late 1800s American shingle style. All major rooms and bedrooms face the water and the sections of the house that would have overlooked the neighbor's house now look out to the sea.

The ample rooms feature 11-foot ceilings; the house's overhanging eaves diminish direct sunlight. The identical octagonal breakfast room and winter/summer porch are set at the two ends of the house with an open kitchen/family room, dining room, music/living room, and library/office set along the spine. The four family bedrooms upstairs follow the water and are accessed off a curved hall. The only rooms without views in this 7,300-square-foot house are the first-floor guest bedroom and the playroom above the garage.

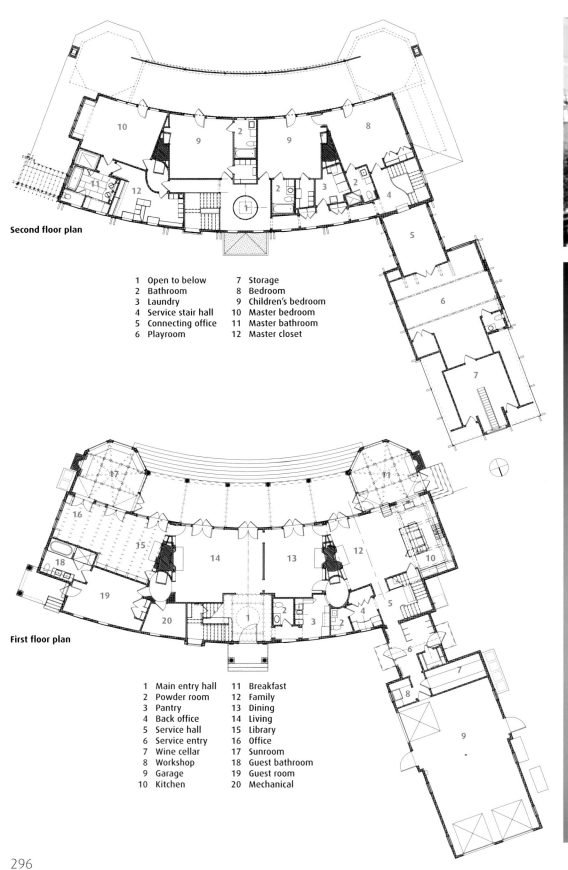

Second floor plan

1	Open to below	7	Storage
2	Bathroom	8	Bedroom
3	Laundry	9	Children's bedroom
4	Service stair hall	10	Master bedroom
5	Connecting office	11	Master bathroom
6	Playroom	12	Master closet

First floor plan

1	Main entry hall	11	Breakfast
2	Powder room	12	Family
3	Pantry	13	Dining
4	Back office	14	Living
5	Service hall	15	Library
6	Service entry	16	Office
7	Wine cellar	17	Sunroom
8	Workshop	18	Guest bathroom
9	Garage	19	Guest room
10	Kitchen	20	Mechanical

Omarapeti House

Wairarapa, New Zealand

Bevin + Slessor Architects

Photography: Paul McCredie

This house was designed to accommodate self-sufficiency in energy use and to utilize sustainable practices wherever possible. Decisions regarding water supply, hot water heating, space heating, waste treatment, solar control, insulation, ventilation, materiality, and the selection of appliances, fixtures, and fittings were made according to sustainable principles.

The simply formed, individually clad "boxes" congregate around a combined cooking, eating, and living space. Each living and sleeping area has access to an elevated outdoor deck area. The self-contained guest "box" can be closed off and separately accessed.

The house is constructed of materials selected for their combination of durability and texture as well as their contribution to a more sustainable method of building. Materials include doubled-glazed aluminum joinery, oil-stained weatherboard, oil-stained battened plywood, Zincalume roofing, cement plastered blockwork, FSC-certified hardwood decking, plantation-grown interior timber flooring and plywood ceilings, and salvaged native timbers for bench tops.

Landscaping around the house consists of recently unearthed river boulders, crushed river gravels, and natural pasture grass regrowth. To avoid the need for garden and/or lawn maintenance, sheep are allowed to graze right up to the house perimeter, placing this building unequivocally in its rural setting.

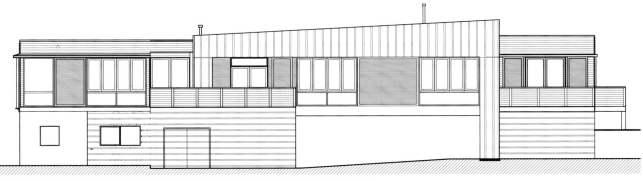

Northeast elevation

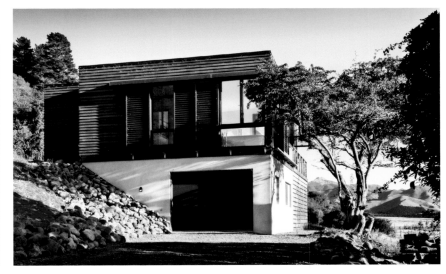

299

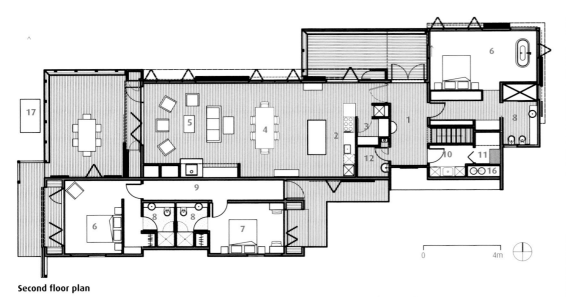

Second floor plan

1 Entry hall
2 Kitchen
3 Pantry
4 Dining
5 Living
6 Bedroom
7 Bedroom/study
8 Ensuite
9 Side hall
10 Laundry

11 Storage
12 WC
13 Water storage
14 Garage
15 Battery room
16 Gas bottle/woodstore
17 Solar hot water panel

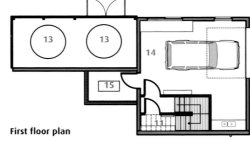

First floor plan

0   4m

Osler House

Brasilia, Brazil

Marcio Kogan + Studio MK27

Photography: Pedro Vannucchi

The plan of this house is based on a ground floor volume, a suspended volume, and a deck with an outdoor pool. The concrete and wood box on the ground level houses the master suite, a bedroom, bathroom, the utilities area, and the garage. Vertical wooden brise soleils filter the light and can completely open the rooms to the outside, dissolving the relationship between internal and external spaces. The upper volume, supported by the ground-floor volume on one side and by pilotis on the other, accommodates the living room, the kitchen, and a small office.

An exterior staircase connects the deck alongside the pool to the upper solarium. An indoor staircase forms the daily circulation of the house. Near the main circulation, in the foyer of the house, is a specially designed panel by Brazilian artist Athos Bulcão, possibly his last work and a great privilege for the home owner and the architects. The brise soleils, the pilotis, and the plan with two perpendicular volumes work together in this house as a commentary on the modern architecture of Brasilia.

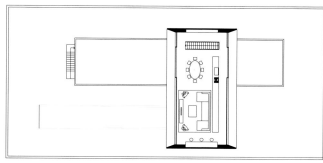

Second floor plan

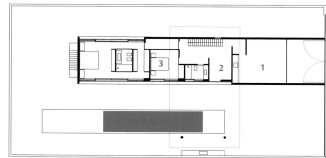

First floor plan

1 Parking
2 Hall
3 Guest room

0   9m

303

Paddock House

Blair Atholl, South Africa

AMA Architects

Photography: Dalton Dingelstad

The architecture of this farmhouse at Blair Atholl is a response to the rural African location. The precious nature of the site, with its animals, vegetation, and rural neighbors, challenged the architects to "touch the earth lightly."

The home is dwarfed by the surrounding trees that line the paddock; it sits at the end of the paddock vista, opening its façade fully to the beauty of its remarkable surroundings. Abundant windows, including narrow floor windows and enormous double-volume shopfronts, bring these surroundings deep into the house. The interior materials are a simple yet warm combination of white walls and ceilings, Lauro Pretto timbers, powder-coated aluminum windows, off-shutter concrete soffits, porcelain ceramic floor surfaces, woven light fittings, and leather. The owners' significant collection of artworks is an integral part of the interior materials palette.

This family home celebrates abstraction, simple and contemporary elements, and modern geometric form within a rural vernacular that is seen in the paddock fencing, stonework, grassed hills, pebbled streams, and views to the horizon, forested enclaves, and a spectacular night sky.

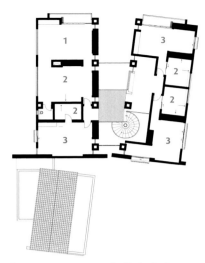

Second floor plan

1 Master bedroom
2 Bathroom
3 Bedroom

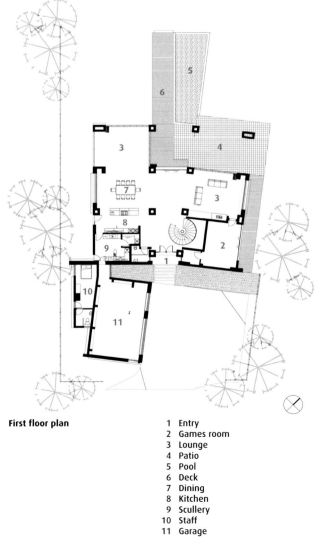

First floor plan

1 Entry
2 Games room
3 Lounge
4 Patio
5 Pool
6 Deck
7 Dining
8 Kitchen
9 Scullery
10 Staff
11 Garage

Panoramic House

Bregenz, Austria

K_M Architektur

Photography: courtesy K_M Architektur

The location of this family home near Bregenz, with a clear view of Lake Constance and The Alps, is unique. The site, on the slope of a green meadow, offered perfect conditions to design a house that captures, through its form, the natural features of its surroundings.

While the house sits on a solid concrete foundation, the upper part of the building was constructed from wood. A loggia encircles the building on the "view side," fulfilling the owner's desire for an open living space. This loggia connects all the rooms on the upper floors and creates a flowing transition between interior and exterior. The effect is intensified by sliding floor-to-ceiling glass doors on this side of the façade. Deep overhangs over the loggia provide protection from the sun and elements. The back of the house appears to be more closed, though a small set of outside stairs enables direct contact with nature at all times.

The outer skin of unpainted wood encloses the many openings and views and unites the building, despite its interplay of open and interior spaces.

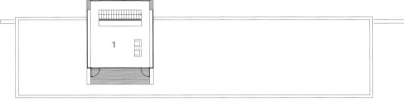

Third floor plan

1 Library

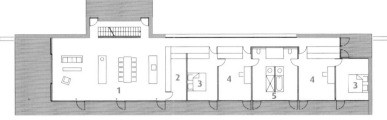

Second floor plan

1 Kitchen/dining/living
2 Pantry
3 Bedroom
4 Study
5 Bathroom

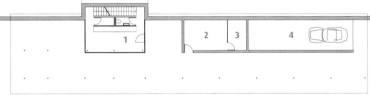

First floor plan

1 Entry
2 Wood storage
3 Mechanical
4 Garage

0   8m

Parabola

Setagaya, Tokyo, Japan

Yasuhiro Yamashita/Atelier Tekuto

Photography: Makoto Yoshida

This long, narrow site is located in a quiet residential area surrounded by nature. The site is elevated 10 feet above the road level so that on clear days, it provides views of Mount Fuji.

As the family spends much of its time in the living room, this room was situated on the top floor so it can benefit from the scenic views. In order to fully exploit the length of the site, the top floor cantilevers over the front of the building.

Minimal design and a parabolic ceiling on the top floor are the building's distinctive features. Splashes of color provide a contrast to the undulating white surroundings, giving rhythm to the space. The flowing "three dimensional" ceiling, which dips and rises to varying heights, arouses contrasting feelings of tension and release and gives the rooms a sense of immense space. The fluctuating density invokes a sense of movement, which unconsciously guides the observer right through and beyond the rooms' boundaries. While normally the floor and the walls delineate the boundaries of an interior space, in this case, it is the parabolic ceiling that defines its essence.

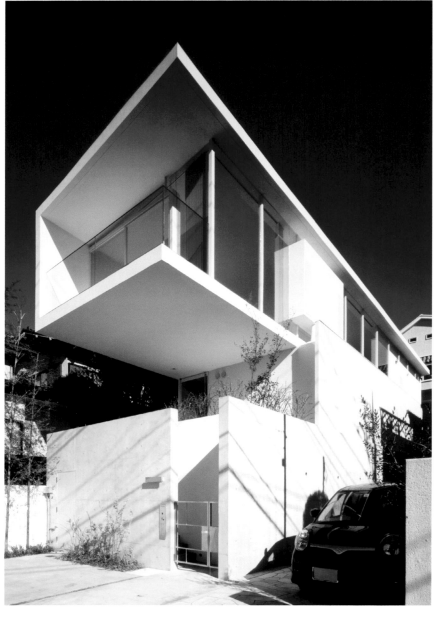

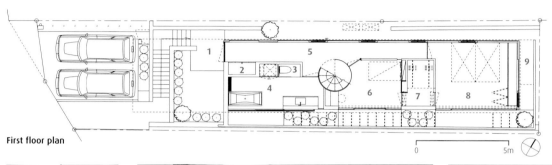

Second floor plan

First floor plan

1	Terrace
2	Living
3	Dining
4	Kitchen
5	WC
6	Storage
7	Spare room
8	Service terrace

1	Entry
2	Shoe closet
3	WC
4	Utility
5	Hall
6	Children's room
7	Walk-in closet
8	Bedroom
9	Closet

0   5m

Piedra Roja House

Santiago, Chile

Riesco + Rivera Arquitectos Asociados

Photography: Sebastián Wilson León

The architectural concept for this house was based on the traditional houses of central Chile, in which a variety of patios play an important role in daily life. The house was conceived as a solid horizontal concrete plinth with the steel structure attached; glass and ventilated partitions are added.

The house is a north–south-oriented rectangle into which patios are inserted according to different programs and their uses. The plan is divided into three longitudinal strips: the first contains the bedrooms and a long corridor oriented to the north and the garden; the second contains services such as circulation, storage, and bookcases and is oriented to the south; in the center, the third strip contains the public spaces and the patios.

A "hard" patio separates the living and dining rooms; a "green" patio separates the living room from the children's area, injecting humidity to control high temperatures; a "playground" patio for the children relates the children's area to the garden; and finally, a "working" patio relates to the kitchen and the garage areas.

The roof is conceived as an expansive, empty horizontal element that allows air to circulate through the walls to the ceiling, and then is expelled through ventilation chimneys.

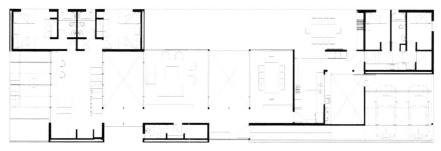
First floor plan

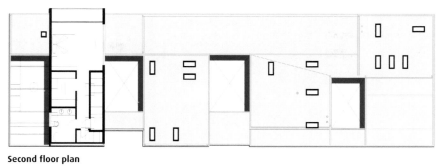
Second floor plan

313

Quinta Da Serra

Portugal

Adam Richards Architects

Photography: Timothy Brotherton

This house is located in a national park in southern Portugal. The area is characterized by simple agricultural buildings with mono-pitched roofs and by stone field walls and jagged terraces that cling precariously to the dramatic, mountainous landscape. The brief was to reconstruct a house on the footprint of the original derelict farmhouse on the site.

The existing stone walls were rebuilt and a new earthquake-resistant concrete-frame box-like structure was built within the walls. New white-rendered wings spin out from this box, enclosing bedrooms and defining courtyards.

The house is divided into two elements. The stone box of the main block is imagined as a kind of clearing, an orthogonal walled enclosure whose high ceiling suggests an abstracted sky. Within the clearing, two narrow strips forming a cross in plan overlap each other over three stories—these contain elements such as stairs and kitchen equipment. The cross shape divides the spaces, defining different sized areas that contain the principal activities for living, dining, cooking, and working. The spaces that lead to the clearing have the character of the mountains in a dramatic spatial sequence. The house culminates in an over-scaled chimney, emphasizing the symbolism of the hearth, and setting its face against the harsh weather.

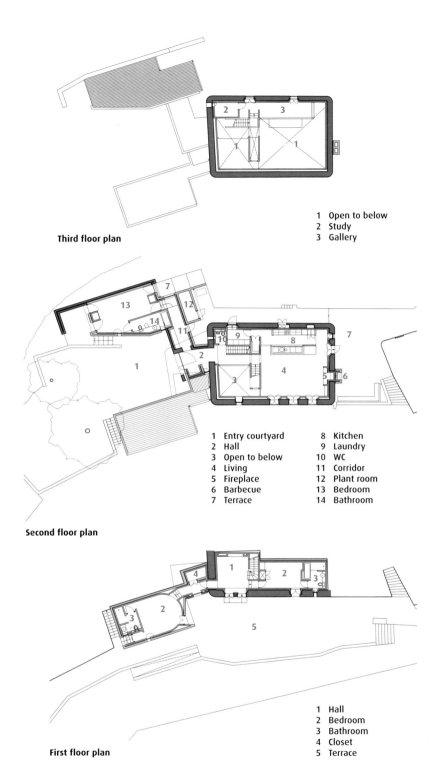

Third floor plan

1 Open to below
2 Study
3 Gallery

Second floor plan

1	Entry courtyard	8	Kitchen
2	Hall	9	Laundry
3	Open to below	10	WC
4	Living	11	Corridor
5	Fireplace	12	Plant room
6	Barbecue	13	Bedroom
7	Terrace	14	Bathroom

First floor plan

1 Hall
2 Bedroom
3 Bathroom
4 Closet
5 Terrace

Redmond Residence

Seattle, Washington, USA

FINNE Architects

Photography: Benjamin Benschneider, Nils Finne, and Paul Warchol

This house, on a 3.5-acre wooded hillside site with large stands of fir and cedar, is a delicate structure of wood, steel, and glass, perched on a stone plinth of Montana ledgestone. The stone plinth varies in height from 2 feet on the uphill side to 15 feet on the downhill side.

The major elements of the house are a living pavilion and a long bedroom wing, separated by a glass entry space. The living pavilion is a dramatic space framed in steel with a "wood quilt" roof structure. A series of large north-facing clerestory windows create a soaring, 20-foot-high space, filled with natural light.

The interior features many custom-designed fabrications, including complex, laser-cut steel railings, hand-blown glass lighting, bronze sink stands, miniature cherry shingle walls, a textured mahogany/glass front door, and unique furniture such as the cherry bed in the master bedroom. The dining area features an 8-foot-long custom bentwood mahogany table with a blued steel base.

Sustainable design features include extensive clerestory windows for natural lighting and cross ventilation, low-VOC paints, linoleum flooring, 2 x 8 framing to achieve 42 percent higher insulation than conventional walls, cellulose insulation, radiant heating, and natural stone exterior cladding.

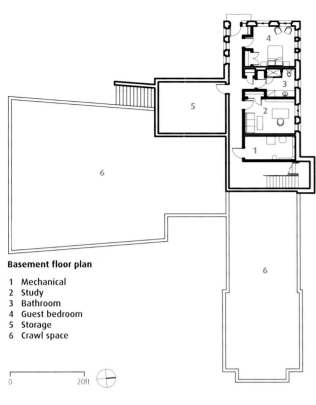

Basement floor plan

1 Mechanical
2 Study
3 Bathroom
4 Guest bedroom
5 Storage
6 Crawl space

0   20ft

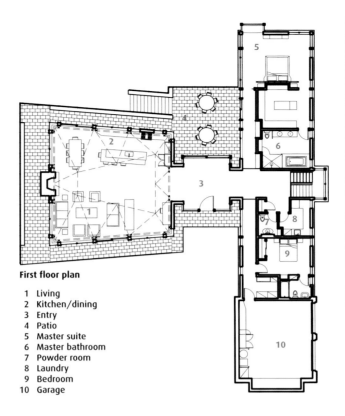

First floor plan

1 Living
2 Kitchen/dining
3 Entry
4 Patio
5 Master suite
6 Master bathroom
7 Powder room
8 Laundry
9 Bedroom
10 Garage

Residence for a Briard

Culver City, California, USA

Sander Architects, LLC

Photography: Sharon Risedorph
Photography

This 3,800-square-foot house was named for the owners' dogs, a French breed known as the Briard. The structural frames, exterior walls, and roof were all prefabricated off-site by warehouse manufacturers, shipped to the site on one flat-bed truck and then simply bolted together. Once the shell was complete, all interior walls, systems, and finishes were completed in a traditional manner. The warehouse frames allowed for a generous scale for the interior spaces: the great room, for example, has a 28-foot ceiling.

The sculptural southern façade design was derived from a painting of a violin by Braque ("Aria of Bach," 1913). This was especially appropriate as

the client is also a music critic, who requested that the house be a place where string quartets could come and play for an audience. To accommodate this, the great room is surrounded by a suspended balcony. The long side of this balcony is a shallow stairway with treads that are wide enough for two chairs side-by-side. The handrails are transparent glass, with grasses laminated into the lower half of the glass to allow for a view of the musicians below.

The home is a showcase of green residential architecture with its extensive use of ecological/sustainable materials, systems, and strategies.

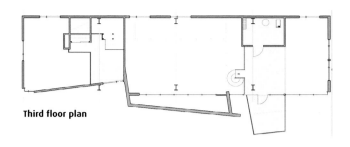

Third floor plan

Second floor plan

First floor plan

0   20ft

Residence Schlüter

Karlsruhe, Germany

Meixner Schlüter Wendt Architekten

Photography: Christoph Kraneburg

This family home is on a generously proportioned site in Waldstadt, a 1960s residential estate located in a pine forest. The immediate vicinity is characterized by abundant pine trees, large sites, and single-family homes in a mix of styles.

The architectural concept was to explore the relationship between the dwelling and the natural surroundings and to introduce reciprocal spatial flows between the indoors and outdoors. The architects considered the principles of space and mass, particularly of space as "deducted mass" that results in the open intermediate areas of the house such as loggias, terraces, and the entrance area.

The design is based on the allocation of functional areas and the admittance of maximum natural light. The form of the building, in particular the roofing over the loggia area, controls the incidence of light during the day and over the year. In spring and autumn when the sun is low, the sun shines into the living area. In summer, the structure of the building shields the interior from the heat of the sun so there is no necessity for sun protection or air conditioning.

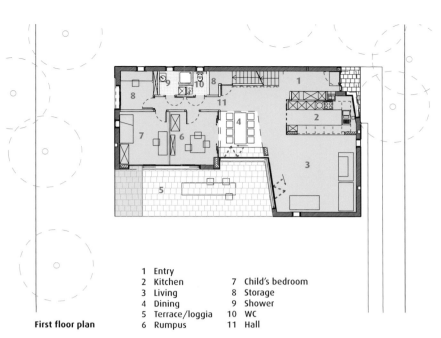

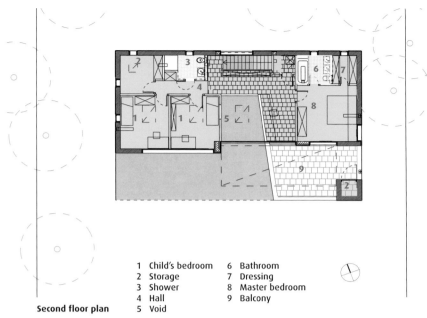

1 Entry
2 Kitchen
3 Living
4 Dining
5 Terrace/loggia
6 Rumpus
7 Child's bedroom
8 Storage
9 Shower
10 WC
11 Hall

First floor plan

1 Child's bedroom
2 Storage
3 Shower
4 Hall
5 Void
6 Bathroom
7 Dressing
8 Master bedroom
9 Balcony

Second floor plan

Riddell Road House

Glendowie, Auckland, New Zealand

Pete Bossley Architects

Photography: Simon Devitt

This house is designed to take advantage of the site and cater for the busy lifestyle of the owners and the constant comings and goings of their extended family and friends. It is planned around a pivotal central space that welcomes visitors, extends the lounge space for large gatherings, and connects the different parts of the house together horizontally and vertically. A curved wall of fine vertical cedar battens rises up through the space from the basement level and defines one edge of the atrium.

This central space is also the climate control for the house. Large panels of Anthra Zinc at the upper level automatically open when the space reaches a certain temperature to ventilate the atrium and the spaces beyond and close automatically if the temperature drops or it starts to rain.

The exterior spaces are an extension of the interior; large sliding doors open up the atrium, lounge, and dining spaces to honed concrete terraces on either the seaward or pool side of the house. An outdoor room with fireplace extends the lounge space to the pool.

Robust, textural materials include Anthra Zinc cladding, basalt ashlar stone, cedar battens, recycled ironbark sunshades, French oak flooring, plywood ceilings and cabinetry, and honed concrete terraces.

1 Entry
2 Formal lounge
3 Dining
4 Family sitting
5 Kitchen
6 Pantry
7 Laundry
8 Office
9 WC
10 Linen/coats
11 TV room
12 Bathroom
13 Guest bedroom
14 Garage
15 Tool store
16 Outdoor room
17 Pool
18 Family terrace
19 Service court
20 Entry bridge
21 Viewing platform
22 Office
23 Lounge
24 Main bedroom
25 Ensuite
26 Closet
27 Walk-in linen closet
28 Bedroom
29 Bathroom
30 Bridge
31 Catwalk deck
32 Deck
33 Void

Second floor plan

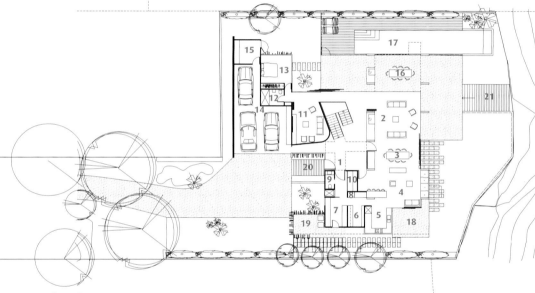

First floor plan

Rising Glen Residence

Los Angeles, California, USA

Janna Levenstein/Tocha Project

Photography: Michael McCreary Photography, www.havenstudio.com and Katarina Malmström, www.katarinamalmstrom.com

This residence is grounded in true formal characteristics, which are offset by expressive geometric imbalances that stimulate unpredictability. Strong sight lines were formed by setting walls, floors, and ceilings to draw away and toward each other in unison. Greenery was cultivated into the home's spaces and planted to enliven the floors and walls of bath areas. To encourage circulation, water features and pathways glide throughout the home. At the entry, a path of original 1950s terrazzo leads from outside to inside and around the main body of the home to adjacent rooms that branch off from the path.

The kitchen hosts a massive monolithic island of poured polyurethane that radiates from inside to the outside cooking area. The bar (also polyurethane) features a hinged oversized window that gracefully tucks to the side, permeating the outdoor space.

Carefully customized thin profile bi-fold glass doors reflect the inside and outside environments. A variety of exotic woods are used for cabinetry, wall veneers, and sinks to add warmth and balance against the pristine doors. These warm wood tones, along with rich, muted color tones amplify the spaciousness and elegance of the space while fueling a contrasting rhythm of bold and subtle in this modern habitat.

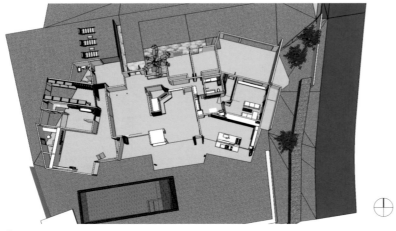

Floor plan

Robinson House

Auckland, New Zealand

Tim Dorrington Architects

Photography: Emma-Jane Hetherington

This major transformation grew from an original brief that included adding a pool pavilion adjacent to the existing pool. Added to the brief were a transformation of the exterior presentation, reconfiguring the interior spaces, and re-presenting and re-planning the grounds around the house.

The main house now features black stained board and batten gabled "sheds" in homage to the rural setting, and to blend more with the natural aspects of the site. Internally the house was completely re-planned and finished giving more appropriate priority to the size and layout of individual spaces.

The new pool pavilion is designed as a roof plane sitting lightly on a stone landscape wall at one end and an oversized steel frame at the other. The stone wall steps and continues around the pool area, containing the space. The pool is centered in the courtyard and appears to have scooped out of the stone. The water level of the pool matches that of the surrounding stone tiles, while the pavilion floor hovers slightly above to provide housing for the pool cover.

The three glazed walls of the pavilion can be completely opened up, allowing maximum flexibility in the usage of the space to suit weather conditions.

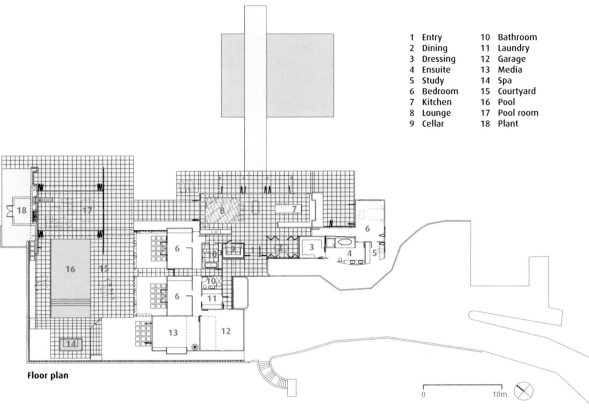

1	Entry	10	Bathroom
2	Dining	11	Laundry
3	Dressing	12	Garage
4	Ensuite	13	Media
5	Study	14	Spa
6	Bedroom	15	Courtyard
7	Kitchen	16	Pool
8	Lounge	17	Pool room
9	Cellar	18	Plant

Floor plan

0   10m

335

Rota House

Madrid, Spain

Manuel Ocaña

Photography: Miguel de Guzman

The client, a well-known veteran actress, commissioned the architects to completely refurbish this dark terrace-type dwelling in the center of Madrid. Her dream was to have a swimming pool at home, as well as a loft with an elevator, and abundant natural light.

The single-fronted property faces north on a narrow and dark street, but the prime part of the house is at attic height, facing south, with wonderful views of the roofs of Madrid's historic center.

Simple demolition work allowed the three levels to be flooded with natural light; the swimming pool now occupies the space of the former courtyard.

A challenge was to insert 700 cubic feet of water at 99 °F (37 °C) into a domestic program of some 14,000 cubic feet. This demanded a thorough climate conditioning study and, importantly the active participation of the owner, who must operate the four devices that are incorporated to control and condition the temperature and humidity of the interior spaces. Passive air conditioning is achieved through cross-ventilation. The lower level is waterproof: floors, walls and ceilings are painted with white chloride rubber and the sheet staircase is treated with marine varnish.

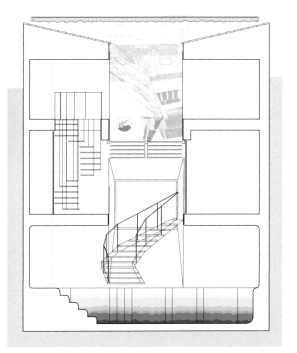

337

Rubin Residence

Bloomfield Hills, Michigan, USA

McIntosh Poris Associates

Photography: Kevin Bauman

This residence, designed for an empty-nester couple, rests on the edge of a ravine. From the street, the house appears as a single-story ranch home surrounded by lush landscaping. Inside, the house virtually opens up to nature through the vast wall of windows in the back, giving endless views of the woods and ravine and abundant natural light into the open living–dining area. Cut-out windows throughout the house frame the natural setting, bringing it into the home almost as artwork.

The main floor encompasses areas used on a regular basis such as the master suite, kitchen, living room, dining room, and den. With few walls separating individual rooms, the space is organized instead by functional objects such as a dual-purpose quilted leather wall that faces the living area and a cantilevered wood-clad table-top, attached to a storage unit, that separates the kitchen, living, and dining rooms.

The lower level looks out to the large courtyard and Zen garden and the ravine beyond. In the courtyard, a set of stairs rises along a cedar-clad volume to an unattached screen porch and terrace, providing additional space for outside dining and entertaining. The stairs are lined with glass railings for uninterrupted views.

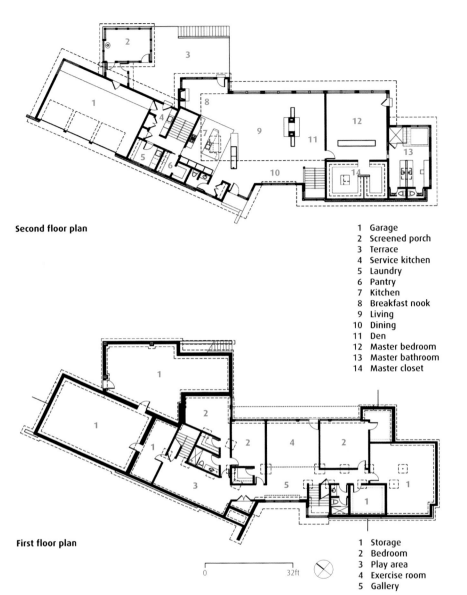

Second floor plan

1 Garage
2 Screened porch
3 Terrace
4 Service kitchen
5 Laundry
6 Pantry
7 Kitchen
8 Breakfast nook
9 Living
10 Dining
11 Den
12 Master bedroom
13 Master bathroom
14 Master closet

First floor plan

1 Storage
2 Bedroom
3 Play area
4 Exercise room
5 Gallery

0   32ft

Ruddell House

Kauai, Hawaii, USA

Moore Ruble Yudell Architects & Planners

Photography: David O. Marlow

This house, on the majestic north shore of Kauai, is shaped by the unique local and regional landscape characteristics. The property is part of a working farm perched on the rim of a coastal valley, overlooking the dramatic north shore coastline.

Climate considerations played a central role in the form and function of the house, which is situated on a southwest-facing bluff with valley and ocean views. The house is composed around the natural topography of the site and is organized as a series of pavilions that are connected by loggias, courtyards, and passageways.

The clients' desire for a union between inside and outside is realized in the way open spaces alternate with building masses along a circulation spine. Exterior spaces vary in size, character, and orientation.

The house functions to filter the eastern trade winds, optimizing natural ventilation and framing local and regional views. Deep overhangs provide shelter from the harsh tropical sunlight, while clerestory windows at the top of the pavilions capture soft light.

The colors and materials used reflect those of the sky and local flora and respond to the light and landscape to celebrate the cycles of nature. The building, landscape, and inhabitants are woven into a dynamic yet harmonious composition.

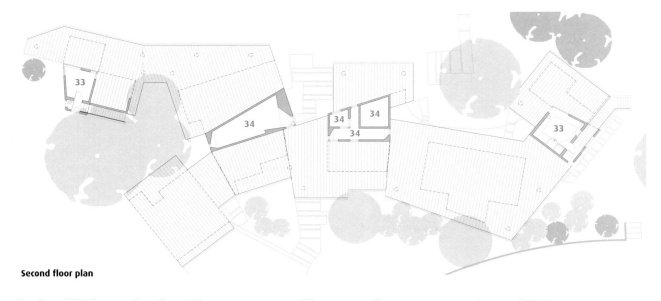

Second floor plan

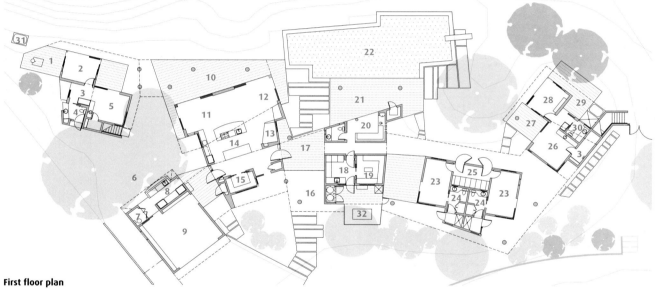

First floor plan

1 Outdoor shower
2 Master sleeping bay
3 Closet
4 Master bathroom
5 Master bedroom
6 Outdoor dining
7 Storage
8 Outdoor kitchen
9 Garage
10 Outdoor deck
11 Dining
12 Living
13 Punea (Hawaiian bed)
14 Kitchen
15 Office
16 Entry porch
17 Entry gallery
18 Laundry
19 Dressing room
20 Cabana
21 Spa deck
22 Pool
23 Bedroom
24 Bathroom
25 Common area
26 Guest bedroom
27 Deck
28 Guest sleeping bay
29 Outdoor guest shower
30 Guest bathroom
31 Outdoor bathtub
32 Outdoor treatment spa/shower
33 Studio
34 Open

0   25ft

Rutherford House

Oruatua, New Zealand

Tim Dorrington Architects

Photography: Emma-Jane Hetherington

While spectacular, the location of this house, bordered by the Taupo Tauranga River and close to Lake Taupo, had some associated risks. A flood plain covers the site, requiring minimum floor levels of almost 3 feet above ground level.

The brief was to create a modern holiday house suitable for the hot summers of Lake Taupo and the cold winters for skiing on Mt Ruapehu.

The house has four main elements: a concrete base, which at some points is folded up to contain interior space; two black cedar-clad bedroom blocks; and a white structured "veranda," which one of the black boxes appears to slip under.

The concrete base provides the required floor level above ground to suit flood plain requirements and provides the opportunity for intermediate zones between inside and out. Raised decks from both the main living room and the second lounge create elevated and—in the case of the front deck—covered outdoor spaces.

The living space incorporates several layers of space to suit differing climates, activities, and degrees of privacy. The kitchen, lounge, and dining areas are in a large open-plan "veranda." An adjoining "snug" with fireplace can be closed off from the main space. The top-floor sitting room provides a private space to retreat to.

Second floor plan

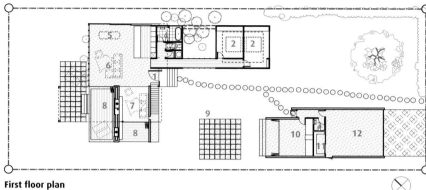

First floor plan

San Agustín

San Pedro Garza García, Nuevo Leon, Mexico

RDLP Arquitectos

Photography: Arq. Jorge Taboada

This house is open toward all four sides, permitting maximum transparency, views, and light through the clever interplay of windows and blinds. Interior spaces are shaped by a series of screens of differing heights and positions, which determine uses and circulation patterns. On the ground floor the entrance, living and dining rooms, the study, and the service areas are blocked or extended through walls, terraces, fountains, blinds, and patios.

The three bedrooms, the family room, and two very large terraces—one with views to the street and the other to the neighboring stream at the back of the house—are on the second floor. The ground-floor entrance is connected with the family room on the second floor through a double-height space. The arrangement of the spaces makes them appear larger, both vertically and horizontally, and visually connects them with the stream and the surrounding landscape.

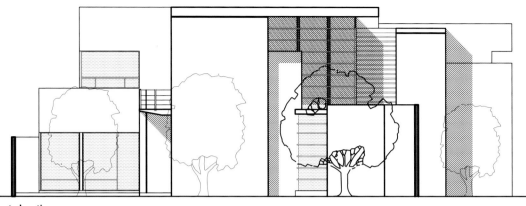

East elevation

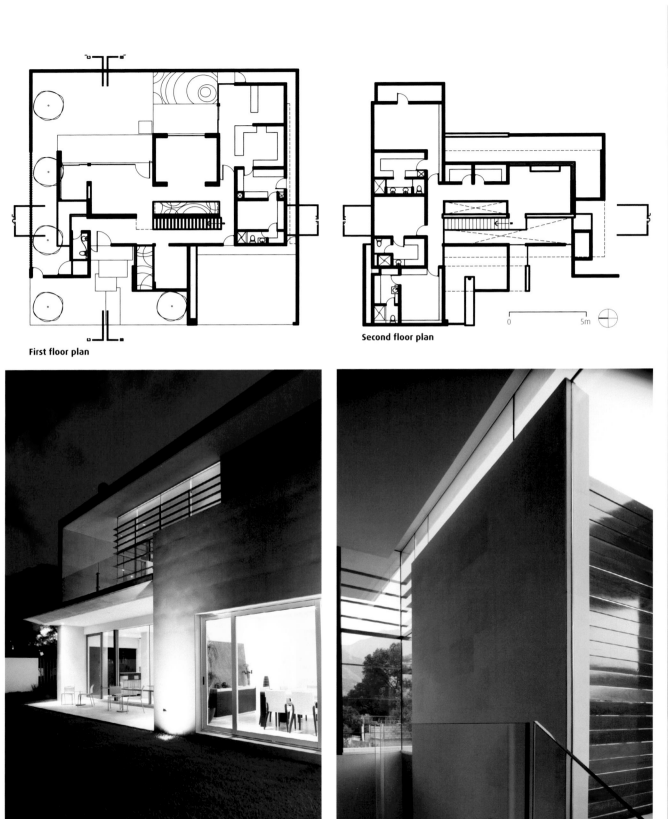

First floor plan

Second floor plan

0 5m

Screen House

New Westminster, British Columbia, Canada

Randy Bens Architect

Photography: Roger Brooks

The brief was to add a new floor to an existing 1954 bungalow in a post-war neighborhood that is rich with modernist architecture. The existing house was an L-shaped bungalow that was too small for a growing family. The new floor, the domain of the parents, contains a studio, master suite, and two decks. Architecturally, the goal was to knit together the old and new with simple gestures and materials that would be sympathetic to their context, yet fresh.

Stacking the new program on top of the old resulted in a mass that was neither vertical nor horizontal. To counter this, and to shade the south-facing living room, a horizontal screen was introduced to give the composition a more restful and balanced appearance. The screen extends past the living room in both directions, creating a covered entry to the east and an open structured space to the west. To further reinforce the horizontality of the screen, a concrete planter/plinth/address wall was introduced at the ground plane.

To blend old and new, bright rolled zinc panels were placed above and beside existing window openings. Simple aluminum trim serves as a datum for window heads, mullions, and sills, and is present on all façades.

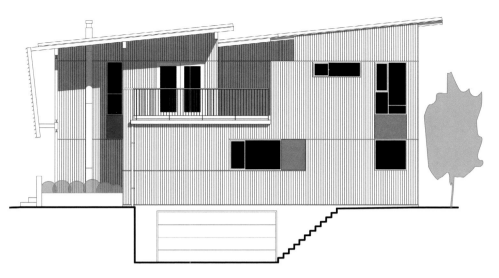

Sherman Residence

Mill Valley, California, USA

Lorcan O'Herlihy Architects

Photography: Tim Griffith

This 4,200-square-foot house sits on a south-facing hillside on a ridge overlooking the upper Tamalpais Valley and San Francisco Bay beyond. The complexities found in the natural landscape and topography of Mill Valley, with its spiraling movement of folded planes and steep hillsides, established dynamic conditions critical to the direction of the overall design of the house.

Complexity came in the tethering of the house to the hill. The primary level, which houses the main public spaces, is visually anchored to the site as it bends in plan along natural contour lines. Simultaneously, the house cantilevers over the precipitous incline, its main floor supported by horizontal steel beams. The beams attach to the rear wall, reinforced for additional strength. In the rear, the house stands on steel columns with diagonal bracing embedded in concrete foundation beams. A composition of floating rain screen wood skin and smooth troweled plaster is used innovatively on the exterior skin to further articulate the geological conditions of the surrounding valley.

The upper volume folds in section and in plan, creating a dynamic dialogue with the main level. This level houses the glass-walled master bedroom suite that has panoramic views of the San Francisco Bay.

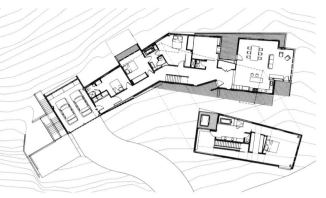

First floor plan

Shop House

Singapore

ONG&ONG Pte Ltd

Photography: Derek Swalwell and Tim Nolan

The ornate art deco façade of this former shop house gives no clues to the contemporary residence it shelters. Inside, a metallic architectural language unifies the spaces and conveys a modern flavor.

The overall scheme successfully establishes a relationship between inside and outside spaces and presents a diverse series of spaces suited to a range of activities. A large aluminum-clad airwell divides the two sections of the house, allowing maximum light penetration and encouraging natural ventilation.

The ground floor features flexible glazed walls that lead directly to the central pool, alongside which an old frangipani tree grows through a wooden deck. The main spiral staircase is a rhythmic ribbon that ascends to the attic space and acts as a central pin through the main section of the residence. On the second and third floors, the stairwell is encased in a stainless steel mesh. A cylindrical roof skylight above creates a vertical column of light that can reach the bottom part of the stairs.

The master bedroom features an ensuite bathroom in the form of a glazed box that cantilevers over the pool area, and a large void that allows views down to the first floor. These modern interventions emphasize the playful nature of the scheme.

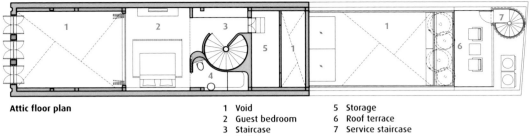

Attic floor plan

1 Void
2 Guest bedroom
3 Staircase
4 Bathroom
5 Storage
6 Roof terrace
7 Service staircase

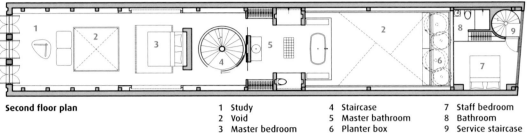

Second floor plan

1 Study
2 Void
3 Master bedroom
4 Staircase
5 Master bathroom
6 Planter box
7 Staff bedroom
8 Bathroom
9 Service staircase

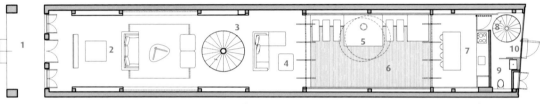

First floor plan

0   5m

1 Walkway
2 Living
3 Staircase
4 Pool lounge
5 Courtyard garden
6 Pool
7 Open kitchen
8 Service staircase
9 Powder room
10 Rear entrance

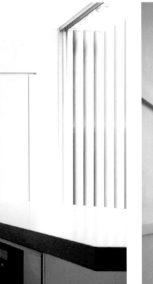

Simon Residence

La Jolla, California, USA

Safdie Rabines Architects

Photography: Undine Pröhl

This family residence is located in a canyon, perched above the ocean. The house steps up from the street toward the canyon summit and is divided into two parts that are connected by a glass vestibule. The main part of the house curves along the canyon's edge, allowing ocean views from each room, while the guest rooms, art studio, and garage are located in a rectangular block toward the street. As the house wraps around the site, it creates an internal southern courtyard protected from the ocean winds.

The entrance sequences from both the street and the garage follow the slope of the site. A winding stone path climbs to the front door and squeezes between two walls, the wood wall of the front house, and the curved plaster garden wall. The entrance vestibule links the different areas of the house, both inside and outside, offering the first glimpse of the canyon and the interior courtyard on arrival.

The ceiling in the main house curves up toward the canyon, while a low ceiling along the circulation provides space for clerestories and a more intimate scale for the house. The single-story structure hugs the landscape, allowing the dramatic canyon and ocean views to take center stage.

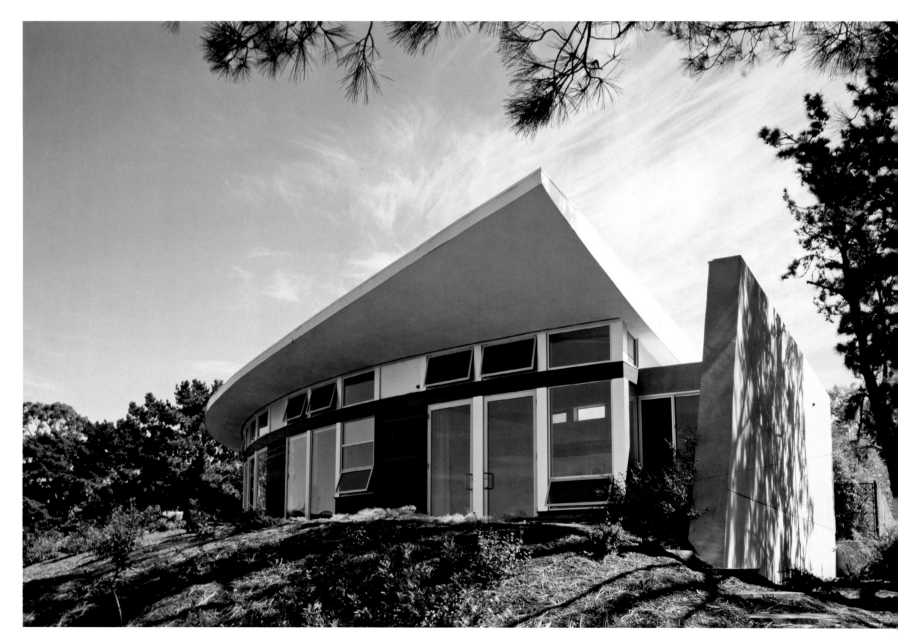

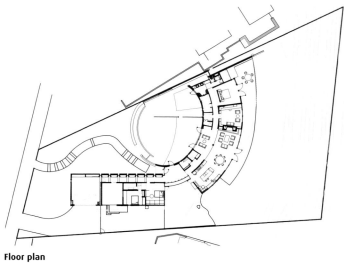

Floor plan

Stern Residence

Palm Beach, Florida, USA

Mojo Stumer Associates

Photography: Mark Stumer

This 7,500-square-foot residence was designed around the clients' need for a complete living plan on the ground level. The program is quite extensive since both occupants needed private working spaces in close proximity to the master bedroom on the ground level. They also required that all the rooms on this level be connected via internal doors, so that they could open the rooms up to one another for informal living, while being able to close them for formal use and entertaining. All the guest spaces are on the second level.

The extensive use of copper on the exterior barrel vault will not only wear well under adverse heat and driving rain conditions, but also gives the house a unique look. The copper roof details give the elevations a sculptural, contemporary effect while helping the house blend with its traditional Spanish tile-roofed neighbors.

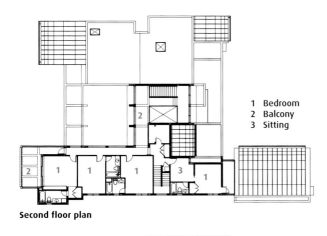

Second floor plan

First floor plan

Sunrise

Prahran, Victoria, Australia

Jolson

Photography: Scott Newett Photography

This 1950s confectionery factory has been transformed into a superb contemporary home and architect's studio. The old saw-tooth factory roof was removed, leaving a concrete slab between the first and second floors. The concept was to build an elevated house, set back from the street façade to create a large north-facing private garden.

The industrial and slightly raw appearance of the ground-floor space contrasts against the more refined solution of the residential component above. Both spaces, however, are equally sophisticated where the spaces, elements, and finishes are controlled to offer seamless function and circulation.

On the second floor three large rectangular blocks have been inserted into the space and contain and conceal the functional aspects for living. A large image depicting the sugar vats making "hundreds and thousands" confectionery has been enlarged to reflect the history of the building. This image slides to reveal the functioning kitchen. A 20-foot Zimbabwe granite island bench reflects the surrounding flat surfaces in the kitchen. The third level contains the sleeping accommodation, bathrooms, and gym.

The informal living areas overlook the large private garden. The garden acts as a thermal buffer to the ground-floor office, retaining heat in winter and providing insulation from the summer sun.

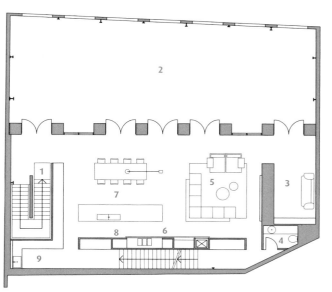

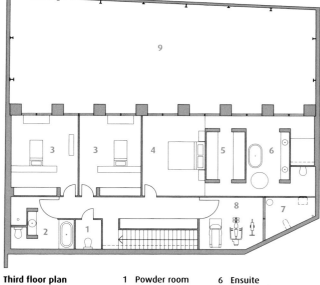

Second floor plan

1	Main entry stairs	6	Sliding screen
2	Grassed area	7	Dining
3	Playroom	8	Kitchen
4	Powder room	9	Laundry
5	Lounge		

Third floor plan

1	Powder room	6	Ensuite
2	Bathroom	7	Courtyard
3	Bedroom	8	Gym
4	Master bedroom	9	Void
5	Walk-in closet		

0   5m

Swan Street Residence

Perth, Western Australia, Australia

Iredale Pedersen Hook Architects

Photography: Peter Bennetts

For this major renovation and extension, the architects explored ideas of time and context through the appropriate use of material and form derived from historical studies, combined with a careful consideration for how the building may weather and change as a continuing dynamic experience. Time is abstracted through the use of green film and polycarbonate, or actively encouraged by the contrasting weathering of timber, or anticipated by the slow process of oxidization of the copper trims. Context was considered in relation to the arts and crafts movement in Perth at the turn of the century, the immediate suburb, and the specific house.

Sustainability principles are present on multiple levels, beginning with retaining the original house rather than demolishing it and therefore preserving the streetscape. The roof was developed with wide eaves to shade both levels of windows and then folds down as a parasol wall, reducing heat loads from the hot western sun while allowing cool southwest winds. Walls are constructed from reverse brick veneer with a layer of wool insulation. Timbers are either recycled or from Australian managed forests. Internal walls are painted white to maximize the reflectivity of the surface.

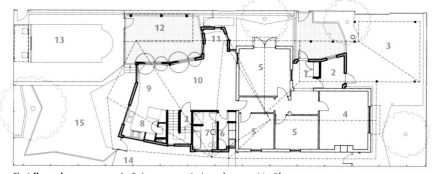

First floor plan

1	Entry	6	Laundry	11	Play area
2	Storage	7	Bathroom	12	Deck
3	Carport	8	Kitchen	13	Existing pool
4	Lounge	9	Dining	14	Drying court
5	Bedroom	10	Living	15	Lawn

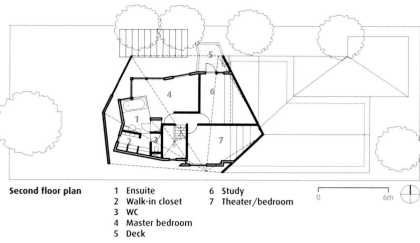

Second floor plan

1	Ensuite	6	Study
2	Walk-in closet	7	Theater/bedroom
3	WC		
4	Master bedroom		
5	Deck		

0   6m

Temple Hills Residence

Laguna Beach, California, USA

LPA, Inc.
Schola

Photography: Costea Photography, Inc.

The design of this house—a remodel of a 1950s post and beam cottage—is a study in connections. Taking its cues from the eclectic neighborhood, the design captures the essence of the original cottage, and reinterprets the traditional post and beam into a unique residence. The resulting solution is a house of two faces connected through a thin sheet of glass.

Nestled into a steeply sloping 5,000-square-foot site the volumes step up the hillside to create a series of ascending spaces. While the two existing box-like structures create a base, the addition exploits the openness and modular nature of post and beam connections. A monolithic concrete block mass anchors the addition. Structure and glass pinwheel off the mass, creating dematerialized living spaces that continually open up to the views.

At the heart of the sustainable strategies employed is the reuse of the entire existing home. In addition, solar orientation, deep overhangs, and operable glass allow the house to breathe with little mechanical assistance. The palette is a mix of renewable and exposed building materials, eliminating the need for secondary finishes.

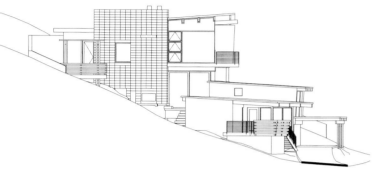

Third floor plan

Second floor plan

1 Carport
2 Living
3 Dining
4 Kitchen
5 Study
6 Bedroom

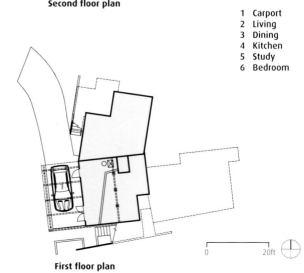

First floor plan

0   20ft

Thirty-one Blair Road

Singapore

ONG&ONG Pte Ltd

Photography: Tim Nolan

This contemporary renovation of an Art Deco style terrace house has a minimal, industrial ambience. It is an innovative response to the heritage building constraints, which included retaining most of the existing elements of the building envelope, and retaining the height of the second floor. To overcome this, the ceiling was raised to accommodate additional space in the roof by inserting a mezzanine level on the second floor. To resolve lighting issues, a jack roof now allows large amounts of light in through the attic space and to the mezzanine.

A folded steel-sheet staircase hangs elegantly from a suspended I-beam at the top of the house. This sculptural circulation space services the main part of the house while a rear steel spiral staircase leads up to a guest bedroom and a roof terrace.

A large internal courtyard bisects the house, not only providing flexible inside/outside space, which encourages natural ventilation, but also allowing light to penetrate both sections of the house.

The master bedroom at the top of the house has been designed with a connection with the childrens' room below, reiterating the concept of continuity between each space. Each bedroom has full-height window shutters along one wall that are similar to the traditional exterior shutters.

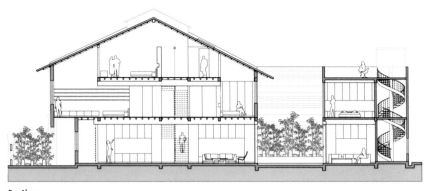

Section

375

1   Master bedroom
2   Central staircase
3   Master bathroom
4   Void
5   Courtyard
6   Roof terrace
7   Barbecue pit
8   Aircon ledge
9   Rear staircase

Attic floor plan

1   Bedroom
2   Walk-in closet
3   Bathroom
4   Central staircase
5   Laundry
6   Courtyard
7   Rear staircase

Second floor plan

1   Walkway
2   Open kitchen
3   Staircase
4   Living
5   Courtyard deck
6   Family
7   Rear staircase
8   Powder room
9   Rear entry

First floor plan

0   5m

Todos Santos House

Baja California Sur, Mexico

Gracia Studio

Photography: Sandra Muñoz

This project is in Todos Santos, a small town one hour south of La Paz Baja California Sur. The challenge was not only the design but the technical aspects and cost efficiency given the lack of available labor and high cost of construction materials. The decision was made to train local workers and to use only materials that were available in the small "pueblo" with just two hardware stores.

The project consists of two almost identical houses, one for the owner, and the other for beach rental. A single-story design allows 180-degree ocean views and an indoor–outdoor area as the heart of the house. The 3,400-square-foot houses each have three bedrooms and two bathrooms. The main kitchen, dining, and living areas open to the pool, terrace, and beach views.

The houses comprise two basic materials: exposed concrete walls that match the color of the surrounding sand and "Talavera" tiles, which have been a typical material in Mexico since the Spanish conquest.

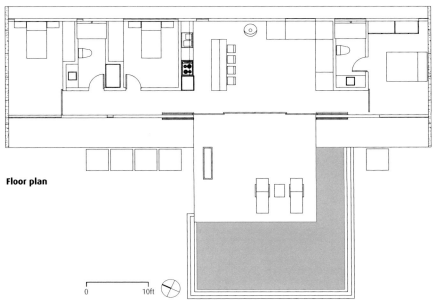

Floor plan

0　　　　　10ft

Tree House

Los Angeles, California, USA

Standard

Photography: © Benny Chan/fotoworks

Built on a steep hillside, this 1,800-square-foot treehouse combines the drama of the setting with the sheltered comfort of a modest cabin. The site, accessible only on foot, meant that design components had to be small enough to be carried up the slope manually by workers.

With its interior spaces layered from back to front, the house is wide open to the tree-shaded southern exterior, yet private in relation to the surrounding homes. A large ash tree surrounds the house, creating an exterior microclimate and dappled sunlight in the interior for most of the year.

On the lower level, living areas combine smooth concrete floors, natural plaster ceilings, and a central redwood-clad wall. Through the redwood wall, the long kitchen and its minimal white cabinetry are visible in the background. A large, full-height sliding door allows the patio and living areas to flow together under the tree. Walnut stairs lead to walnut floors on the upper level, where bedrooms open to the tree's canopy through large wood doors.

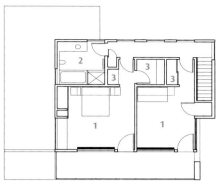

1 Bedroom
2 Bathroom
3 Closet

Second floor plan

1 Entry
2 Dining
3 Living
4 Kitchen
5 Den
6 Bathroom
7 Bedroom

First floor plan

0   20ft

Two Rock Reef House

Abaco, The Bahamas

Susan Maxman, FAIA, SMP Architects

Photography: Barry Halkin Photography

This house complex sits on a white sand cove looking east at the Atlantic Ocean. It is designed to provide shelter in inclement weather while enjoying the stunning views. Its simple painted white interiors of southern pine and sand-colored porcelain tile floors allow the natural beauty of the place to dominate.

The house is composed of two small buildings: the main house consists of a great room with kitchen, dining, and living areas stretched along the beach. A cottage contains a study on the first floor and a master bedroom upstairs.

On this barrier island all resources must be shipped in by barge so it was essential that the house be highly resource-efficient. A tilted roof sloping southwest allows for solar panels to be laminated to the standing seam metal roof. Potable water, collected by the roof, is stored in cisterns under the house. Gray water is recycled for irrigation. The landscape is an integral part of the house design with pergolas and trellises incorporated to allow for vines to climb on and shade the house from the western sun. All the vegetation is native and the beach dune has been restored with sea oats, bay cedar, sea lavender, and sea grape.

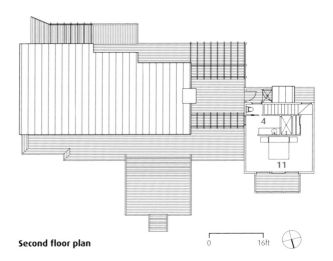

Second floor plan

0 ————— 16ft

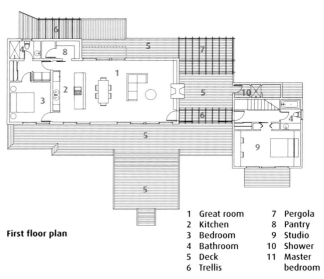

First floor plan

1	Great room	7	Pergola
2	Kitchen	8	Pantry
3	Bedroom	9	Studio
4	Bathroom	10	Shower
5	Deck	11	Master
6	Trellis		bedroom

Vancouver House

Vancouver, British Columbia, Canada

Bing Thom Architects

Photography: Nic Lehoux

The required deep site setbacks on this corner site created an opportunity to develop a significant "garden room" that provides privacy and becomes a tranquil focal point for this residence.

The open plan of the 6,000-square-foot house seamlessly organizes the various activity areas, with living on the ground level, sleeping on the second level, and a play area in the basement. The two-story house is set over a koi pond and forges a symbiotic relationship with the immediate landscape through its serene palette of exposed concrete, glass, wood, and stone. Simple massing, a high degree of transparency, and an expressive roof structure help the interior spaces merge with the immediate surroundings.

Extensive use of architectural concrete on the exterior walls expresses solidity, protection, and tranquility. The application of "stressed-skin" technology on the main roof achieves both structural efficiency and a dynamic roofline. With the same zinc material rendering the top, soffit, and ceiling, the roof becomes a dynamic three-dimensional object that flows above the glass clerestories. A three-story curtain wall anchors an interior court, bringing light and views into the center of the house and the basement. Glass bridges and hanging stairs are carefully detailed to express their materials and structure.

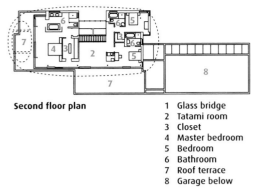

Second floor plan

1 Glass bridge
2 Tatami room
3 Closet
4 Master bedroom
5 Bedroom
6 Bathroom
7 Roof terrace
8 Garage below

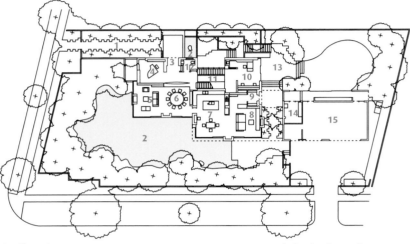

First floor plan

1 Front entry court
2 Pond
3 Entry
4 Piano
5 Living
6 Dining
7 Kitchen
8 Family
9 Rear entry
10 Studio
11 Glass bridge
12 Washroom
13 Stone patio
14 Workroom
15 Garage

Basement floor plan

1 Courtyard
2 Recreation room
3 Home theater
4 Storage
5 Laundry
6 Guest bedroom
7 Bathroom
8 Mechanical
9 Lightwell

Vanguard Way Residence

Dallas, Texas, USA

Morrison Seifert Murphy

Photography: Charles Smith

This was the first house completed in a new Dallas neighborhood devoted entirely to Modernism. The irregularly shaped site overlooks a public park and waterway.

The compact, two-story structure essentially extends to the buildable limits of the property. The garage, accessed via an open motorcourt, can double as a photographic studio. Guests enter from the street under a covered porch, which leads to a double-height entry that is illuminated from above. The space compresses just before entering the next double-height volume of the living room, which adjoins the dining space and kitchen. The master bath, dining space, and living space are arranged enfilade about a centerline that leads through a double-height window wall to a sculpture garden and the park beyond. The guest suite above the dining space is organized about this same axis and has its own view to the park and waterway.

The master suite adjoins a walled terrace containing a spa and fireplace. With the sliding panels open, these spaces can be used as one. The powder room, an exquisite space with a unique plan and dramatic presence, is a part of the entry experience.

The entire house is rendered in hard-troweled, white stucco with sealed concrete floors throughout the ground level.

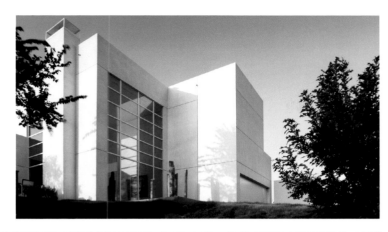

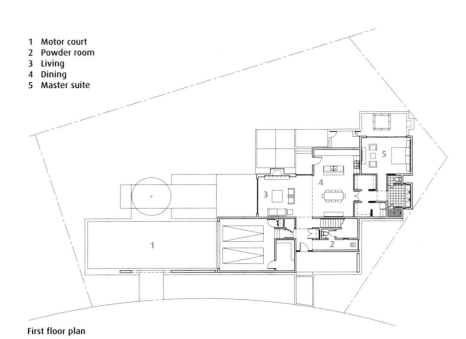

1 Motor court
2 Powder room
3 Living
4 Dining
5 Master suite

First floor plan

1 Media room
2 Office
3 Open
4 Guest room

Second floor plan

0   20ft

Vee House

North Bondi, New South Wales, Australia

Campbell Luscombe Folk Lichtman Architects

Photography: Andrew Worssam Photography and Viewfinder

Situated on the hill behind Bondi Beach, this wedge-shaped site slopes steeply initially, with a substantial level garden at the rear. The steep incline has been harnessed into a terraced garage base to the street, topped by two long pavilions that straddle the side boundaries. They connect via a glazed double-volume entry "gasket." The courtyard between them becomes a focus for the entire dwelling with its 24-meter swimming pool.

Each pavilion is a glazed double-story cube, stepping down to a single story at the rear. A third garden pavilion accommodates the spa, sauna, and *onsen* (Japanese bathhouse). The eastern pavilion has an upper-floor master suite with sea views, with public living on the ground floor.

The media/lounge room, stairwell, elevator, and the children's wing inhabit the ground floor of the western pavilion. Operable walls off the bedrooms orient them to the pool. The upper-floor study accesses both the southern ocean views and the western city skyline. This pavilion is completed with a guest suite and a stairwell to the roof deck.

The glazed double-volume connection between the pavilions is layered with a timber screen and zinc-clad blades. These form a separating device between the formal entry–circulation space and meals area.

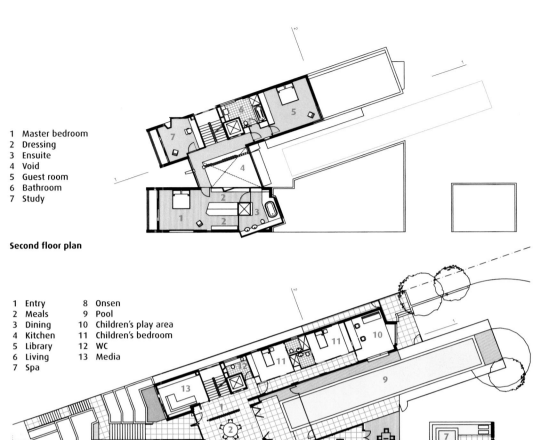

Second floor plan

1 Master bedroom
2 Dressing
3 Ensuite
4 Void
5 Guest room
6 Bathroom
7 Study

1 Entry	8 Onsen
2 Meals	9 Pool
3 Dining	10 Children's play area
4 Kitchen	11 Children's bedroom
5 Library	12 WC
6 Living	13 Media
7 Spa	

First floor plan

Verdant Avenue

Melbourne, Victoria, Australia

Robert Mills Architects

Photography: Trevor Mein and Jonathan Wheatley, Urban Angles Photography

This contemporary three-level inner-city family home is an expression of modernist living. An 80-year-old pin oak tree serves as the focal point for the first-floor living and first-floor bedroom areas, while dominating the third floor library and terrace. A striking sculptural staircase anchors the first to the second and third floors, while glass walls and sliding doors connect the kitchen and living spaces to the garden and 25-meter lap pool outside. Motorized oversize exterior window louvers provide light and ventilation to the entire home. An energy-efficient smart lighting system illuminates the outdoor areas when necessary.

The first floor is largely devoted to the kitchen, living, and dining areas, with a powder room, bathroom, study, laundry, drying room, and cellar. The second level is home to the master bedroom and ensuite, and a further three bedrooms, each with ensuite; plus a living/entertainment zone for the children and a four-car garage at the rear. A theater and library room with extensive city views are at the top of the ribbon staircase on the third floor.

This house dispels the myth that sustainable architecture means sacrificing glamour and luxury. It minimizes its footprint on the land by embracing its external landscape, while celebrating a love for opulent detailing.

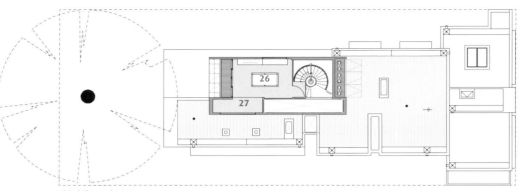

Third floor plan

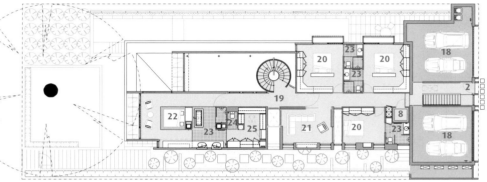

Second floor plan

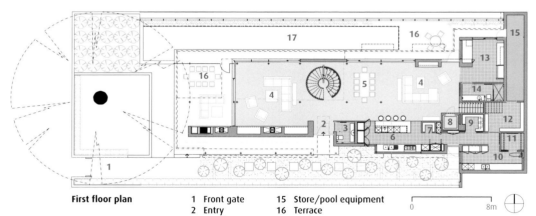

First floor plan

1	Front gate	15	Store/pool equipment
2	Entry	16	Terrace
3	Powder room	17	Pool
4	Living	18	Garage
5	Dining	19	Hall
6	Kitchen	20	Bedroom
7	Pantry	21	Family room
8	Lift	22	Master bedroom
9	Storage	23	Ensuite
10	Laundry	24	WC
11	Drying cabinet	25	Walk-in closet
12	Cellar	26	Library
13	Study	27	Raised platform
14	Bathroom		

0   8m

Vienna Way

Venice, California, USA

Marmol Radziner + Associates

Photography: Joe Fletcher

This residence, designed for a young family, is located on a large, extensively landscaped lot. Floor-to-ceiling glazing and outdoor living spaces fully integrate the home within the California native landscape.

The design divides the narrow lot into thirds, with the two main volumes placed on the exterior edges of the property, bridged by a sunken kitchen in the center. The single-story structure to the south houses a great room that combines formal living and dining areas and flows into an outdoor dining patio. A large expanse of glass along the east provides a visual and spatial link to the pool area.

The northern structure runs from the back of the property forward, also leading to an outdoor living area, and contains more casual, private spaces, including a family room and an office on the first floor and bedrooms on the second floor.

The kitchen acts as the hub of the residence, connecting the public and private areas and providing views of the pool, side yard, and rear property. From the exterior, the kitchen is shaped by a bronze box that emphasizes its significance and provides contrast to the plaster façade found on the main volumes of the residence.

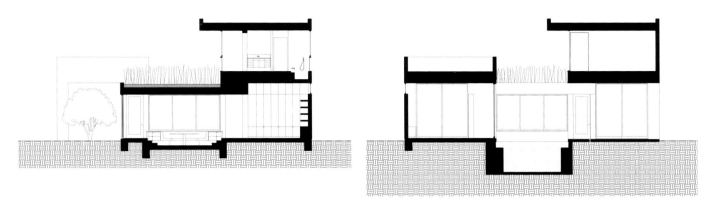

Second floor plan

1 Bedroom
2 Open to below
3 Closet
4 Master bathroom
5 Master bedroom
6 Green roof

0   15ft

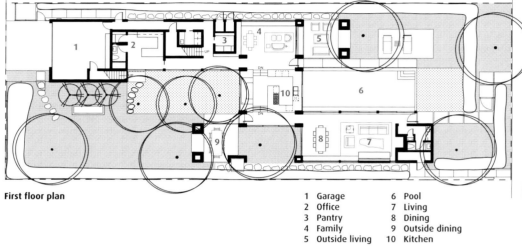

First floor plan

1 Garage	6 Pool
2 Office	7 Living
3 Pantry	8 Dining
4 Family	9 Outside dining
5 Outside living	10 Kitchen

Villa 1

Veluwe Zoom, The Netherlands

Powerhouse Company

Photography: Bas Princen

The Y-shape of this woodlands residence is the result of careful planning to optimize views and sunlight. Half the program is pushed below ground to meet local zoning regulations, creating a dichotomy between the "glass box" ground floor, where the mass is concentrated in furniture elements, and a "medieval" basement where the spaces are carved out of the mass.

In the northeast wing, the rooms are shaped by the nut-wood central furniture piece. In the southeast wing, the kitchen, which receives all-day sun exposure, is shaped by a slate furniture element; the living rooms, shaped by concrete walls, are in the west wing with full exposure to the south. Covered terraces between the sun-exposed wings create natural sun shading.

In the basement level, all rooms are massive and closed, except for carefully positioned windows in the bedrooms. In one wing, the master bedroom is defined by a wooden element that combines the stairs, bath, washing machines, walk-in-closet, and bed. In the other wing, two guest rooms surround the patio, and a vaulted closet-corridor contains all storage. The third wing contains the garage.

The villa's wide array of extreme spatial qualities—from narrow, dark, vaulted corridors to wide-open, transparent garden rooms—results in a landscape that goes beyond the pragmatics of functionality.

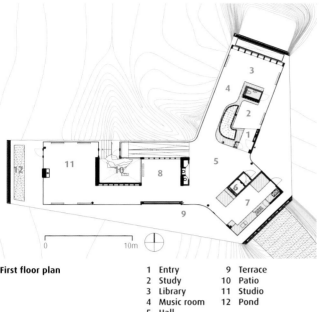

First floor plan

1	Entry	9	Terrace
2	Study	10	Patio
3	Library	11	Studio
4	Music room	12	Pond
5	Hall		
6	WC		
7	Kitchen		
8	Living		

Basement floor plan

1	Garage	6	Guest room
2	Master bedroom	7	Patio
3	Walk-in closet	8	Hallway
4	Bathroom	9	Storage
5	Ramp		

Villa Berkel

Veenendaal, The Netherlands

Architectenbureau Paul de Ruiter

Photography: Pieter Kers

To create openness and lightness and a connection to nature, this house is entirely oriented to the secluded garden at the south of the site. With three of the four façades made of glass, every room looks directly out onto the garden.

To account for the potential lack of privacy created by the glass façades, the site was divided into three long strips at right angles to the road. The bottom and southernmost strip is reserved for the garden, the middle strip contains the villa itself, and the northern strip offers access to the house. This layout of the site means that those parts of the house that the residents prefer to keep private are out of sight.

The layout of the site is echoed in the floor plan of the house. The street side contains the more "public" functions: the entrance, study, kitchen, and living; while the western section, furthest removed from the street, is reserved for the more intimate activities: a corridor that doubles as a TV lounge, the bedrooms, and the bathroom. Each function has its own zone within the house, which can be cut off by means of translucent sliding walls.

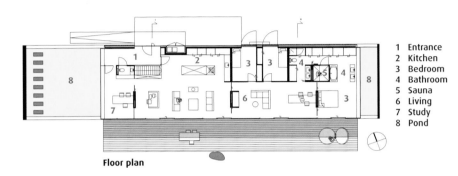

1 Entrance
2 Kitchen
3 Bedroom
4 Bathroom
5 Sauna
6 Living
7 Study
8 Pond

Floor plan

Villa G

Hjellestad, Bergen, Norway

Saunders Architecture

Photography: Bent René Synnvåg and Jan Lillebø/Saunders Architecture

Villa G is a white landmark in the soft landscape of Hjellestad, near Bergen. The house is large yet not dominating, modern but not pretentious. Its futuristic form is built with traditional Nordic materials and architectural elements with a sound basis in Norwegian building methods.

Three different sizes of wooden cladding are mounted in a random pattern on the exterior. An open, covered area on the second floor, which also covers the entrance below, allows for sheltered outdoor living despite the often-turbulent climate.

One of the most interesting features of the house is the stair, which is one solid piece of ⅜-inch-thick steel, galvanized with white sand corn to make it slip-resistant. The stair was produced locally, weighs almost a tonne, and had to be lifted into place by a crane through a window in the roof.

The client, a self-confessed "gadget freak," desired a house with clean lines without any visual noise or clutter. Closets and storage spaces were therefore integrated into "thick walls," about 2 feet deep. The kitchen bench is more than 25 feet long and has plenty of drawers for kitchen equipment and storage. No electrical outlets are visible and a main control panel in the kitchen controls all the technology.

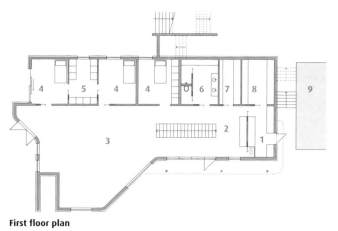

First floor plan

1 Entry
2 Hall
3 Living
4 Bedroom
5 Walk-in closet
6 Bathroom
7 Storage/utility
8 Washroom
9 Garage

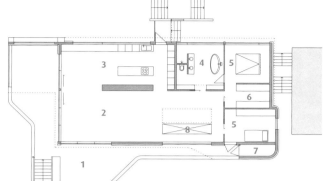

Second floor plan

1 Terrace
2 Living
3 Kitchen
4 Bathroom
5 Bedroom
6 Walk-in closet
7 Storage
8 Opening under skylight

Villa Paya-Paya

Seminyak, Bali, Indonesia

Aboday Architect

Photography: Happy Lim Photography

This villa is used as a holiday home for a family of four and as a rental property for tourists. The site, formerly a papaya plantation and a pig farm, is bordered by a public road to the north and by a *pangkung* (dry river bed) to the south. Its simple program includes a large living and dining area, large staff quarters, a master bedroom with bathroom, and two smaller bedrooms.

The architects wanted to avoid an imposing building; thus the two-level villa appears as a modest single-story building from the road. Behind the simple white box façade, the wooden master bedroom pavilion, with its typical Balinese sloping coconut leaf roof, is an element of surprise.

The massing of the villa follows the traditional Balinese pattern of *natah* or courtyard. Here, the natah is an extension of the open-plan living and dining room, and transforms into a body of water that dominates almost the entire garden, gradually changing from a shallow reflecting pond beneath the cascading entrance step, to the Jacuzzi under the cantilevered balcony, and the main swimming pool surrounding the master bedroom pavilion. The effect is as if the entire villa is sitting on the collection of water (*paya-paya* in Indonesian), hence the name Villa Paya-Paya.

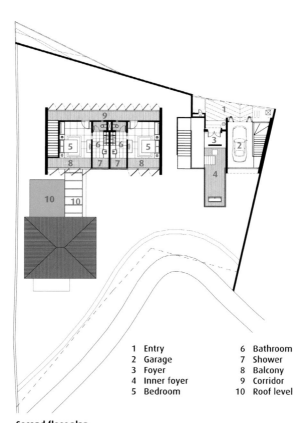

Second floor plan

1	Entry	6	Bathroom
2	Garage	7	Shower
3	Foyer	8	Balcony
4	Inner foyer	9	Corridor
5	Bedroom	10	Roof level

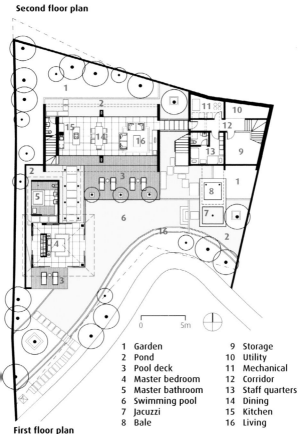

0   5m

First floor plan

1	Garden	9	Storage
2	Pond	10	Utility
3	Pool deck	11	Mechanical
4	Master bedroom	12	Corridor
5	Master bathroom	13	Staff quarters
6	Swimming pool	14	Dining
7	Jacuzzi	15	Kitchen
8	Bale	16	Living

Villa Röling

Kudelstaart, The Netherlands

Architectenbureau Paul de Ruiter

Photography: Pieter Kers

The owners wanted this house to do justice to their extensive art collection. A dilemma arose because of the lakeside location—providing sufficient wall space for the artworks would drastically limit the views. A solution was provided in the form of two contrasting volumes: a transparent glass volume overlooking the lake and the garden, and a "floating" wooden box above for the works of art.

The ground floor consists of a series of spaces that offer varying views of the lake and the surroundings. The glass façade folds itself almost invisibly around the spaces and provides varying amounts of light.

Exterior cloth screens can be extended to protect the interior from solar heat and to create a covered terrace.

The interior spaces are arranged around a central void with a skylight above that allows light to penetrate both floors. Each of the four sides of the upper story features a large window with custom-designed sunblinds, made of horizontal slats, which move like shutters.

Innovative and sustainable temperature regulation is provided by a system of pipes set in the concrete floor. Geothermal power is used to pump cool or warm water through the pipes to heat or cool the house.

Basement plan

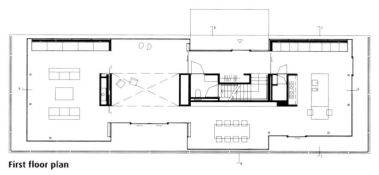

First floor plan

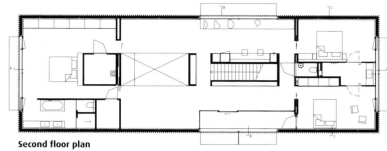

Second floor plan

413

Villa Storingavika

Bergen, Norway

Saunders Architecture

Photography: Michael Perlmutter

Overlooking breathtaking fjords and a stretch of Norway's west coast archipelago, Villa Storingavika is a robust yet refined vessel from which to appreciate the delicate coastline and sometimes rugged climate. The house, a pale timber volume dressed in a crisp, "pleated" dark timber exterior, is oriented along the contours of the site. Concrete stairs link an upper outdoor terrace with a lower lawn, utilizing all of the natural terrain. Built-in concrete furniture increases the use of the lower terrace as an extension of the interior space.

On both stories, the utility and service rooms are located along the northern side of the house, while the living areas open out to the south and the view to the sea. As a consequence, there are very few punctures on the northern side, while large floor-to-ceiling windows face the south. A 20-foot cantilevered balcony, pierced by three circular steel columns, emerges from the landscape-bound volume of the house.

Three main materials are used: glass, black-stained fir, and oiled Canadian cedar. All of the decorative and aesthetic qualities of the building come from the materials themselves and the dimensions of those materials. It is a very elemental, minimal response to the place, and continues through to the simple, robust, and utilitarian details.

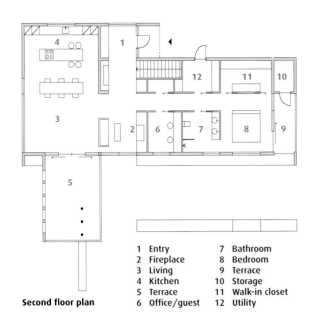

Second floor plan

1	Entry	7	Bathroom
2	Fireplace	8	Bedroom
3	Living	9	Terrace
4	Kitchen	10	Storage
5	Terrace	11	Walk-in closet
6	Office/guest	12	Utility

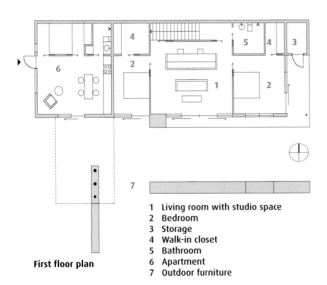

First floor plan

1 Living room with studio space
2 Bedroom
3 Storage
4 Walk-in closet
5 Bathroom
6 Apartment
7 Outdoor furniture

W House

Búzios, Rio de Janeiro, Brazil

Bernardes + Jacobsen Arquitetura

Photography: Leonardo Finotti

This generously sized family house is on a beachfront site. Its location provides privacy from the beach while maintaining unobstructed ocean views from the second-level master suites.

The H-shaped plan divides the house into three axes. On the first axis, gardens are interspersed between the bedrooms and ensuite bathrooms, bringing the exterior environment inside. The second, central axis, acts as circulation, connecting the private areas and the living room. Glass shutters on the side walls of the double-height living room allow natural light to penetrate deep inside the room. A linear swimming pool extends from the center axis to the gourmet kitchen and overlooks the ocean.

Folding wooden shutters and overhanging eaves protect the pool area from the weather and the sun.

A decision to use certified wood influenced both the structural and aesthetic concepts; the entire structure is made from reforested eucalyptus wood laminate without any type of finishing on the beams. The use of various varieties of wood throughout the house unifies the sprawling program and enhances the tropical ambience. Landscaping around the house preserved all the native species on the site while creating pathways that connect the different axes.

Interior design by Toninho Noronha Arquitetura.

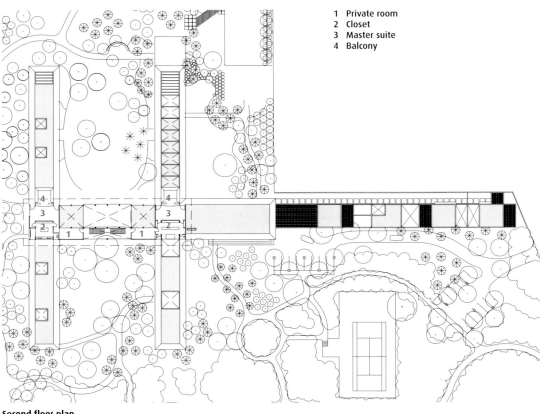

Second floor plan

1 Private room
2 Closet
3 Master suite
4 Balcony

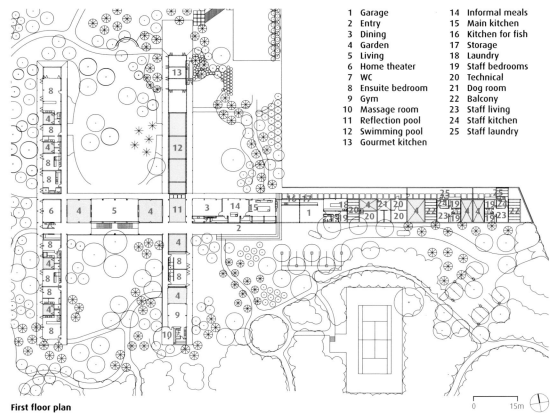

1 Garage
2 Entry
3 Dining
4 Garden
5 Living
6 Home theater
7 WC
8 Ensuite bedroom
9 Gym
10 Massage room
11 Reflection pool
12 Swimming pool
13 Gourmet kitchen
14 Informal meals
15 Main kitchen
16 Kitchen for fish
17 Storage
18 Laundry
19 Staff bedrooms
20 Technical
21 Dog room
22 Balcony
23 Staff living
24 Staff kitchen
25 Staff laundry

First floor plan

0   15m

Weigel Residence

Copper Mountain, Colorado, USA

Substance Architecture

Photography: Farshid Assassi/Assassi Productions

This 4,000-square-foot residence comprises a single-story pavilion containing the primary living and entertainment spaces, and a four-story tower containing the service spaces and bedrooms. The volumes create two distinct landscape experiences: a sequestered, private environment of indoor and outdoor living spaces nestled into the wooded site, and an expansive, open experience of Rocky Mountain vistas afforded by the belvedere quality of the tower.

The northeast entry elevation is largely solid with clerestory windows and a protective cast-in-place concrete wall. Both Interstate 70 and approaching winter storms lie northwest of the site; the garage and interior circulation are used to buffer this side of the home from these environmental factors. The remaining pavilion elevations embrace the wooded surroundings with large glazed openings that blur the distinction between inside and out.

The extended roof overhang creates a large covered exterior deck and shades the glass from summer sun. Fenestration on the tower is limited to a single multi-story opening offering the mountainous panorama to each of the three bedrooms. This simple organization allows the tower to utilize the chimney effect to cool the home in summer months. As a result, the home is radiantly heated, but relies on simple ventilation strategies for cooling.

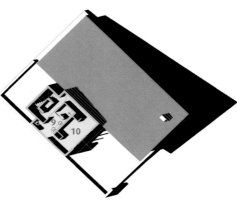

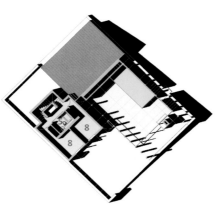

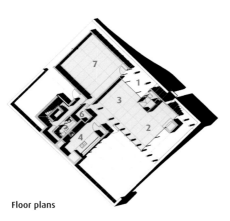

1 Entry
2 Great room
3 Dining
4 Kitchen
5 Bathroom
6 Ski closet
7 Garage
8 Bedroom
9 Master bathroom
10 Master bedroom
11 Office
12 Roof terrace

Floor plans

Westchester House

Scarsdale, New York, USA

Zivkovic Connolly Architects

Photography: Jonathan Wallen

Following the purchase of this 1.25-acre property, the owners decided, for cost, zoning, and environmental reasons, to use the foundations of the nondescript 1950s bungalow that was previously on the site as the starting point for a new family home.

The picturesque new two-story house is a more informal version of a colonial house, with elements common to shingle-style architecture. The owners did not wish the increased bulk of the house to be overstated so kept it modest and relatively intimate in scale. With sensitivity to the environment, the new design retains all the mature trees that were in close proximity to the house.

Also with respect to environmental considerations, in addition to achieving an open, unimpeded feel of space and connection to the outdoors, the house was flooded with natural light by means of four roof lights at the top of the house, as well as bay windows and French doors, which open up the master bedroom directly onto the garden and the eat-in kitchen onto a generous terrace area.

The warmth of the soaring spaces inside is achieved with the use of antiques whose age and history lend character to the respective rooms and sit harmoniously with the family's modern paintings.

First floor plan

1 Entry hall
2 Central hall
3 Dining
4 Breakfast/kitchen
5 Mud room
6 Family
7 Living
8 Bedroom
9 Office
10 Master bedroom

0   20ft

Wexler Residence

Southampton, New York, USA

Mojo Stumer Associates

Photography: Scott Frances

The owners of this 8,000-square-foot shingle-style residence desired a light and airy house that would be a showcase for their extensive art collection. Built on the site of their demolished current residence, the house's exterior architecture blends with its neighbors. Traditional features include the copper turret, stained siding with natural shingles, a herringbone-patterned shingle stair tower, and smooth stone rustication on the lower façade.

Inside, the aesthetic is deliberately modern. The three-story house includes eight bedrooms, eleven full bathrooms, and two half bathrooms. A central great room, featuring 25-foot ceilings, is the focus of the house; a set of triple French doors extend the great room to an outdoor entertaining area paved in bluestone and covered by an extended wood-shingle roof. The kitchen was influenced by the owners' love of gourmet cooking and features commercial-grade appliances, stainless steel drawers and accents, custom cabinetry, access to outdoor areas, and a breakfast nook that overlooks the pool. A multi-use library/den, complete with built-in mahogany bookcases and steel fireplace surround, serves as a relaxing reading room and workspace.

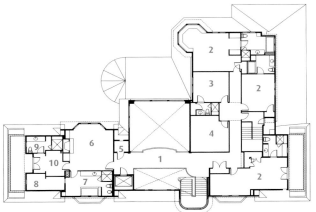

Second floor plan

1 Front hall
2 Bedroom
3 Guest room
4 Exercise room
5 Storage
6 Master bedroom
7 Her bathroom
8 Her closet
9 His bathroom
10 His closet

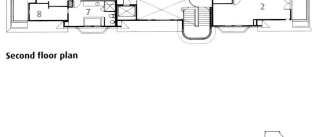

First floor plan

1 Foyer
2 Dining
3 Staff accommodation
4 Garage
5 Breakfast room
6 Kitchen
7 Laundry
8 Outdoor living
9 Living
10 Library
11 Guest room

Basement floor plan

1 Front hall
2 Massage room
3 Storage
4 Mechanical
5 Locked wine room
6 Pantry
7 Sound studio
8 Media room
9 Game room
10 Elevator room

Wheeler Residence

Menlo Park, California, USA

William Duff Architects

Photography: Lucas Fladzinski and Jim Thompson

This 4,850-square-foot house seamlessly integrates sustainable building with modern design. It has four bedrooms, four bathrooms, and a 498-square-foot cabana with a guest room and a bathroom as well as a pool.

The design is governed by a careful system of proportioning based on the Fibonacci sequence. For example, rooms gradually increase in scale from the periphery to the center of the house, culminating in the lofted central family room, which acts as a focal point. Doors that function as "opening walls," continuous concrete floors, and custom casework pieces that define living spaces without fully enclosing them establish flow between different spaces and activities. Likewise, the large corner door system at the family room blurs the distinction between inside and outside. Clerestory windows allow the ceiling to float while drawing in the light and color of the surroundings.

The elimination of interior partitions and the use of custom cabinetry to define functional areas allows for improved natural daylighting of interior spaces, as well as natural ventilation. Economical materials such as fin-ply resin panels, Corten steel, and stained fly-ash concrete establish a dramatic palette of color and texture that celebrates the inherent qualities of the materials, while minimizing the need for maintenance and repairs.

First floor plan

White Ladybird

Shibuya, Tokyo, Japan

Yasuhiro Yamashita/Atelier Tekuto

Photography: Makoto Yoshida

Located in the heart of Tokyo in Shibuya, this house continues Atelier Tekuto's "glass block" series of houses. For this structure however, rather than the glass blocks employed in previous works, steel-reinforced paneling was used. The 6- by 6-inch glass blocks and tiles appear seamlessly embedded in the steel-paneled walls during the day, and in the evening the light emanating from those points makes the whole building look like a glowing ladybird.

The tiles used for the exterior walls were coated with "Microguard," a siloxane-based coating developed in Japan that preserves and protects the pristine condition of the walls. While the floor area of the house is 1,840 square feet, the basement was designed to be easily expandable so that in the future it could be converted into office or shop space.

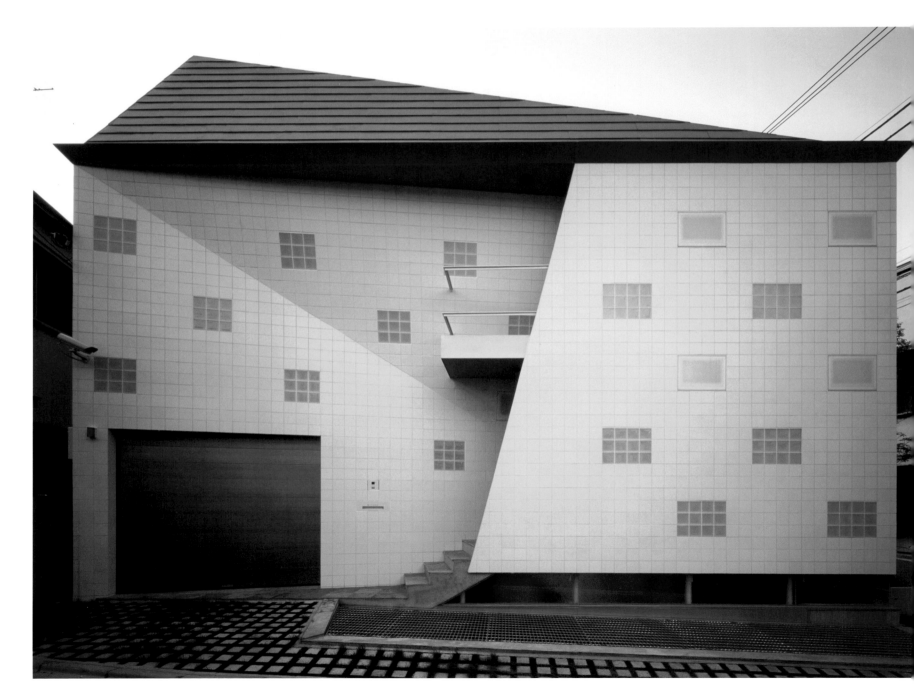

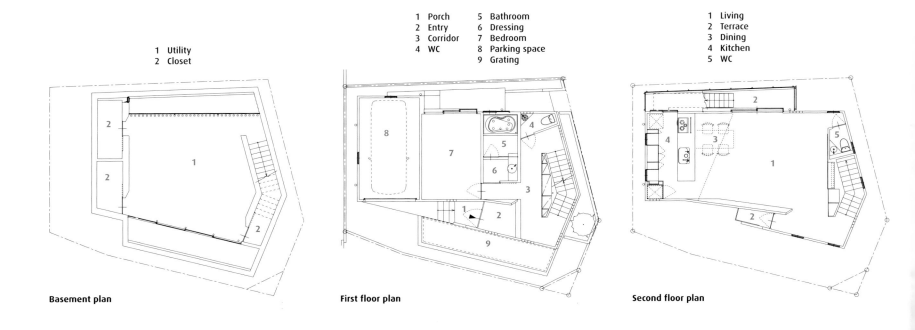

| 1 | Utility |
| 2 | Closet |

1	Porch	5	Bathroom
2	Entry	6	Dressing
3	Corridor	7	Bedroom
4	WC	8	Parking space
		9	Grating

1	Living
2	Terrace
3	Dining
4	Kitchen
5	WC

Basement plan

First floor plan

Second floor plan

Wissioming Residence

Bethesda, Maryland, USA

Robert M. Gurney, FAIA, Architect

Photography: Maxwell MacKenzie

This new house is sited on a heavily wooded lot overlooking the Potomac River, in a rare enclave of modern houses. It occupies the footprint of a pre-existing house in an effort to minimally disturb the site; no mature hardwoods were removed in the process. A new swimming pool is suspended 20 feet above grade to further reduce the impact of the steeply sloping site.

Structural pre-cast concrete planks are employed throughout to expedite the construction process, to span large open areas, and to provide the ability to heat the house hydronically. Combined with a 5-inch concrete slab and terrazzo flooring, the structural system provides additional passive heating. Large overhangs on the glazed southern wall and the tree canopy minimize solar gain in the summer.

Wood siding is combined with soft gray terne-coated stainless steel and black steel window frames to provide an exterior material palette that fits comfortably in the landscape. Bluestone, gravel, and water complete the palette.

Interior materials such as white terrazzo flooring, white oak cabinetry, and aluminum complement the light-filled and minimally detailed space. The creation of this atmosphere refocuses attention outward, allowing the occupants to reconnect with the inherently picturesque site preserved through the design.

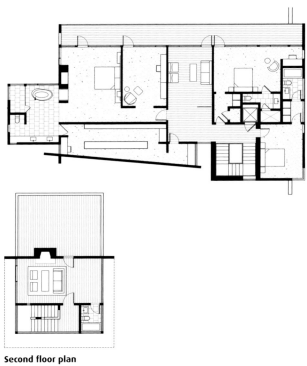

Second floor plan

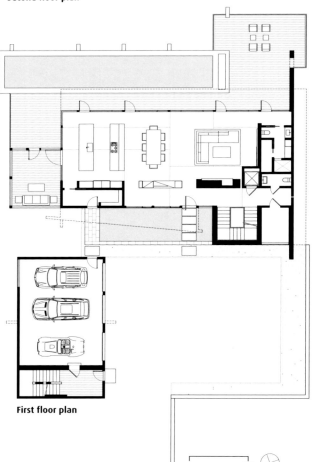

First floor plan

0   16ft

(W)right House

Port Douglas, Queensland, Australia

Charles Wright Architects

Photography: Patrick Bingham-Hall

The architect's intention for this house in Australia's tropical far north was to create an extraordinary landmark that doesn't look like anything identifiable. Conflicting forces and contradictions produce unconventional results and an undeniable public presence, visible from the main road into Port Douglas.

Sustainable design initiatives were critical design generators in conjunction with other conceptual concerns. The entire building opens onto reflection ponds and pools, allowing for evaporative cooling, and has been oriented and further engineered to utilize and control the prevailing winds and summer breezes. To assist with cooling, the whole house works as an aperture for a Venturi effect, allowing accelerated air movement through a constricted opening, demonstrated in both plan and section. Air is pulled through the house by thermal chimneys with mechanically operated vents at high levels forming feature clerestory voids to the articulated plywood ceilings. The house creates its own breezes on the stillest day. The structure is an innovative combination of concrete, steel, and unconventional core-filled clay brick masonry.

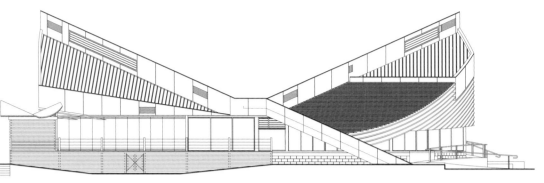

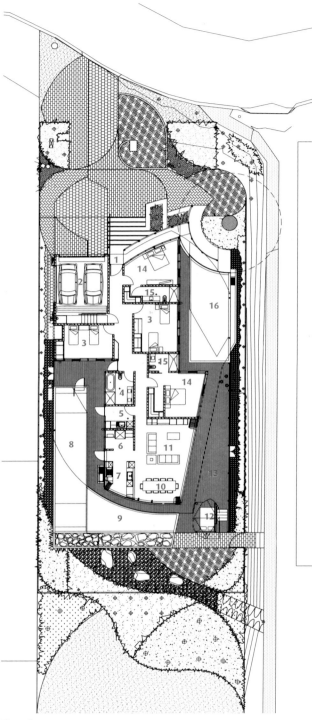

Floor plan

1 Front entry
2 Garage
3 Bedroom
4 Guest bathroom
5 Laundry
6 Pantry
7 Kitchen
8 Swimming pool
9 Wet-edge pond
10 Dining
11 Lounge
12 Daybed
13 External deck
14 Master suite
15 Ensuite
16 Feature pond

YTL Residence

Kuala Lumpur, Malaysia

Jouin Manku

Photography: Eric Laignel and
Roland Halbe

This nine-bedroom, 21-bathroom private residence accommodating three generations of a family—and their guests—encompasses more than 32,000 square feet. It was an opportunity for a young design practice to explore how a new architectural vocabulary could fit with the traditional European architecture commonly used for private houses in Kuala Lumpur.

The entrepreneurial family expressed a preference for the ultra-modern, and was happy to experiment with new shapes, new connections, new awareness of light and sound, and the incorporation of cutting-edge technology.

The residence was conceived in three layers: the base, for public functions; the ring, for guests; and the private house for the family, which is the core of the architectural program. Two levels of floor-to-ceiling glass wrapped in a light louver-system veil of stainless steel, internally clad in chengal wood, are stacked on top of the kitchen, dining, and family rooms that open out to the swimming pool. The internal layout revolves around two vertical axes: one custom-designed circular marble staircase leading from the family and living rooms to the family library and one circular wooden staircase leading up from the kitchen to all family bedrooms. The kitchen lies at the core of the program, anchoring all components visually and conceptually.

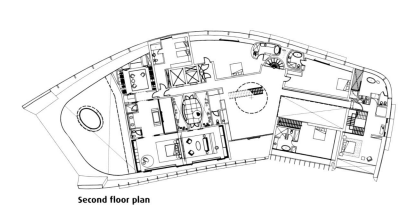

Second floor plan

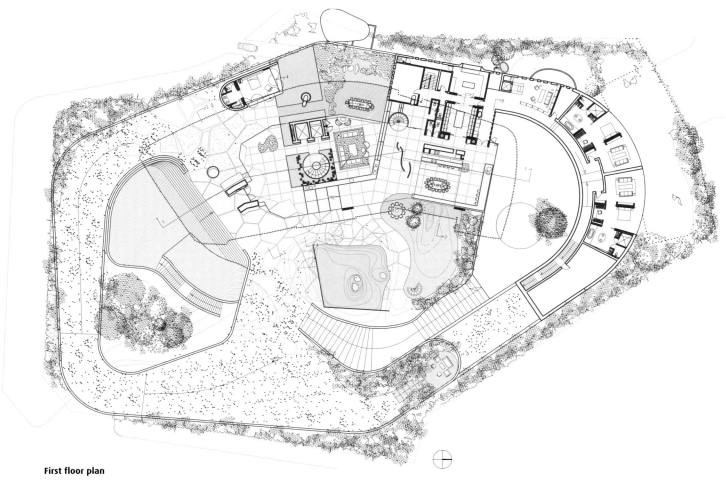

First floor plan

448

Zausner Residence

Bremen, Maine, USA

Barba + Wheelock

Photography: Sandy Agrafiotis

Located on a 30-acre site, this new classic-revival home sits on a high point of land, affording sweeping views of the Medomak River through the trees. The client's desire was for a traditional home, filled with daylight to counteract the long winters and low Maine light. This inspired the architects to integrate innovative features such as borrowed light and a glass block floor, flooded with daylight from the hipped-roof skylit dormers above.

Elegant formal living spaces predominate, book-ended by a rugged dayroom on one end, which serves as guestroom and for casual entertaining, and an English conservatory dining room on the other. Second-floor bedrooms and bathrooms feature other skylit dormers, and the master bathroom triumphs with a full glass shower open to the view. The kitchen, open to the formal living spaces is equally formal, yet functional. Classic proportions and details highlight rooms unified by the recycled old-growth pine floors.

First floor plan

1 Front porch
2 Vestibule
3 Bathroom
4 Dayroom
5 Living
6 Main hall
7 Back porch
8 Dining
9 Conservatory
10 Terrace
11 Kitchen
12 Powder room

Second floor plan

1 Upstairs hall
2 Walk-in closet
3 Master bedroom
4 Built-in alcove
5 Master bathroom
6 Office/library
7 Bathroom
8 Laundry/storage

Index of Architects